This book is dedicated to my wife, Evelyn ("the light")

who reflected the Light of the World, Jesus,

In all of her life and ministry

and as the light of my life,

next to Jesus.

The Zig-Zag Path

To Break The Force of the Hill

William Raymond Kinzie

AuthorHouse™
1663 Liberty Drive
Bloomington, IN 47403
www.authorhouse.com
Phone: 1-800-839-8640

Published by AuthorHouse 03/26/2012

ISBN: 978-1-4685-5111-2 (sc)
ISBN: 978-1-4685-5110-5 (hc)
ISBN: 978-1-4685-5109-9 (e)

ACKNOWLEDGEMENTS

TO

My beloved daughter Rebecca Kinzie Bastian
She spent countless hours of her busy schedule to edit my manuscript. Her suggestions and corrections were priceless. Her MFA in Poetry combined with her expertise as an editor provided extraordinary enhancement to the story. She also created the cover design. Her love for Evelyn and me provided the incentive to do over-abundantly above all that I could ask of her. I love her dearly as did her mother.

My son-in-law, Steven Bastian
As an artist who is competent in Photo Shop, he spent many hours retouching photos and re-doing all of the collages to put them in useable format.

My dear sister Doris Puckett
The author of a best selling book, "In the Hollow of His Hand," about her and husband Larry's forty one years as missionaries in Mexico. She edited and made many important suggestions.

My friend, Pastor Jody M. Link
She also reviewed the book and helped with details about my life as a student at Pennsylvania State University.

PREFACE

When Evelyn and I got married, my wise mother gave us the poem "Zig-Zag Path."

"God leads by the zig-zag path to break the force of the hill."[1]

One of my favorite passages in the Bible is "Trust in the Lord with all your heart and lean not to your own understanding. In all your ways, acknowledge Him and He will direct your path." (Proverbs 3:5-6) This is the story of our lives as we walked that path on our way through life towards the summit.

---

[1] See appendix for the complete poem.

I

Chapter 1

Early Life

"Tip Toe Through the Tulips" murmured on the radio in the birth room when I entered the world. It was October 21, 1929, and my mother was in her bedroom with the doctor while her daughters, Harvena and Ruth, waited anxiously outside. The Great Depression had begun, even there in Catawissa, a small town nestled in the hills of Pennsylvania, but my father, Raymond, was secure for a time in his job as Yardmaster for the Reading Company.

Our house was in front of a cemetery on the top of a hill. In the back yard of this peaceful little town, my father had a vegetable garden and raised chickens. My mother, always caring and industrious, had lost her first husband, Harry, in the coalmines. Harvena and Ruth were only six and eight when their father was killed, but they seemed happy to act as baby sitters for the new addition to the family.

Life was comfortable and in some ways ideal. But a definitive change came into our lives when I was two years old, six weeks after my sister, Doris, was born. As a result of the depression and railroad politics, we had to move for Dad to take a job near Ashland as a railroad car checker, a job he held until he retired. Ashland was a town of 6,000 in the heart of the anthracite coal region. It was situated on a steeply descending mile-long main street. On either side of Center Street, the cross streets all went up. It was almost as if the founders built the main street along a fast running brook between the hills. This became my hometown, the place I stayed until I went to college.

We called our first rental home Devit's after the landlord. A year later, we moved to Eltringham's, where I have my first memories. We lived a few doors from a grocery store on the corner of the block, that when turning right, went down a hill. I liked to sit on the curb at the top of the hill, listening to the blackbirds chattering in the treetops, watching the coal trucks chug by and enjoying the warm summer breeze.

I was taught to say that childish prayer, "Now I lay me down to sleep. If I should die before I wake, I pray the Lord my soul to take"! What a way for a child to be introduced to the reality of death! I was soon to learn that reality could apply to me. One day, Mother and I were on our front porch. She was sitting on a swing swatting flies. "Why are you killing those flies?" I asked. "Flies carry germs that can make you sick" she explained. Mother then asked me if I wanted a piece of hard candy, which I eagerly took. Clutching the treasure in my hand, I asked, "May I go up to the corner to eat it?" "Yes, but do not go out onto the street." I ran past the corner grocery store and sat down on the curb. I was preoccupied with the blackbirds chattering away in the branches, when a fly landed on my arm. To my surprise, I caught the fly and held it between my fingers. With my attention once again on the blackbirds instead of the candy, I put the buzzing fly into my mouth. Alarmed and frightened, I ran back to my mother crying, "Am I going to die? I ate a fly!" Smiling, Mother assured me that no harm would come from eating that fly. It was my very first thought that death could apply to me. I was mortal!

I started pulling practical jokes when I was four. Our house was built on a hill. Mother was doing her washing in the basement with an old wringer washer machine. Three steps down into the yard she would hang the clothes. As I was playing in the backyard, I found a large night crawler worm and placed it on one of the steps to frighten Mother when she came down with a load of clothes to dry. I watched, expecting her to think it was a snake, jump back and scream. To my disappointment, she was not affected in the least.

For the first time, I found out that there were thieves in the world. Dad allowed me to play with his small 22-rifle and I felt like a real cowboy with that. But I left it out on the front porch one night, and it was gone in the morning. Dad was not happy about that! He counseled me, "You must take care of the things you are responsible for!"

Running errands to that little grocery store on the corner was one of my delights. It made me feel like a really big boy. With a list in hand, I would show the grocer what I wanted and when he brought it, I would proudly say, "Put it on our bill."

Dad took me to school on my first day. Up to this time, Doris was my only playmate, so I wasn't used to other children and I had never been in such a formal setting. I was scared. “I don’t wanna stay,” I cried. “I want to go home with you!” “Just stay here in the classroom a minute; I will be out here in the hall,” he replied. I don’t know how long he stayed, but I remained for my first day in school. From then on, it went well, but I don’t have any vivid memories from those early grades. I do remember that I thought a girl with dark hair and pigtails was special, because she was said to have Indian blood in her and I was impressed by stories about the Indians.

Another turn in life came after several years when we moved to “Boyer’s,” a place about three blocks away. It was a duplex on a street that sloped uphill rather steeply. Across the street was another part of the hill that sloped up and away from our home. No houses were built there, so it was a natural place for children to play. We called it “Stormy Hill.” Shirley Boyer was a few years older than the other younger children in the neighborhood, so she became the leader. I still remember the excitement of being on Stormy Hill when someone shouted, “Jack the Ripper is coming!” and we all ran like scared rabbits down the hill for home.

These were reckless times, inviting accidents and injury. Sometimes the older Boyer boys would be on the hill. A gang of the sixth streeters began to throw rocks at us third streeters. We would throw rocks back at them. Unfortunately, since I was about five, my rocks did not reach very far. One day a rock slipped out of Bobby’s hand and hit me on the head, causing a bloody gash.

On another occasion, we were trying to play baseball with a wooden plank for a bat and a teddy bear for a ball. I stood behind the batter as the catcher. The teddy was pitched, the batter missed, but I got caught! A nail sticking out of the plank hit my head and ripped a slice from my nose past my eye into my forehead, another bloody gash!

Days later, when we were playing follow the leader a "tragedy" happened. I was the leader, a position I liked. Round and round I led in our backyard trying to offer the most difficult and dangerous challenges possible. Between our yard and the Boyer's was a wired fence with a narrow frame. The narrow frame presented an ideal challenge. I walked along the top of the fence and Doris tried to follow. To my dismay, she fell and broke her arm. I was not the leader she needed to follow!

One day Dad surprised us with a little puppy, which we named "Queenie." She was a mongrel but she grew to be a pretty dog with an expressive face and short legs. With this new presence in our family, I learned to love animals and I found new responsibilities. She became my buddy. She followed me wherever I went, wagging that bushy tail. But Queenie had a habit of lying under Dad's car. One day Dad jumped in the car to go to work as Mother watched from the front porch. She saw Queenie under the car and called Dad to stop. He did—with a tire right on top of Queenie. He backed off, picked her up and rushed to the veterinarian. Queenie survived, but she growled when we tried to go near her. It was many weeks before she was back to normal. I don't know when I began praying that Queenie would live to be at least seventeen years old, but that tough little dog did live until she was seventeen. I learned that God answers even simple prayers!

My mother taught us to pray the Lord's Prayer and to say the 23rd Psalm and the Apostle's Creed. I can recall how much the Psalm meant to me as I heard her repeat it every night before her prayers. I did not know the full meaning of those beautiful words, but I can remember how brave the words sounded after my mother explained them to me: "Though I walk through the valley of the shadow of death, I will fear no evil, for Thou art with me." I was still afraid of death, even though I knew that there was a God. At night, I knelt by my bed and looked at the picture of Jesus praying in the garden. I felt very close to the Lord at those times.

Mother also taught Doris and me some basic things about honesty and truthfulness. One day when I was with her in a local grocery store, I noticed that some wrapped candy had fallen on the floor. Wanting to be helpful, I picked them up and put them in place, but took one for my effort. That bothered me, and I still remember it. I felt like a thief!

Sunday mornings we went to Sunday School in the Lutheran church. A groundwork in the Word was probably laid there in Sunday School, although I cannot remember any of the lessons I heard. I can recall enjoying the Bible Stories and the wonderful picture presented of Jesus. I also remember the blue and red Scripture cards which we saved until we had enough to win a Bible. But in spite of this background, I do not recall coming to a saving knowledge of Christ during those Sunday School days. However, as a young fellow, I did always call upon God for protection when I was in danger. I prayed for my parents and my animals, believing that God would answer my prayer. But I had not yet become His child.

I also learned about unjust punishment (at least in my eyes). Many Sundays we traveled to my Dad's parents home about twenty-five miles away. Grandmother always prepared a good Sunday dinner. One day I was in the kitchen and was curious about how her drop leaf table worked. As I raised the leaf up and down, I pinched my finger painfully. Grandmother rushed over and instead of comforting me, she slapped my face for playing with her table.

When I was in 3rd grade, still another bend in the road came when we moved up-town. My grandfather had suffered a heart attack and the family decided that we should rent a large home where two families could live. The huge living room was divided with a drape and my bedroom was in the rear half of the room. The rest of our family lived on the second floor and Grandmother and Granddad lived on the third floor. My ill grandfather stayed in bed all the time. I don't remember how long he lived, but I remember the sad and unpleasant funeral. As I gazed upon his cold, dead body, I felt again the fear of death. For a long time after the funeral, the smell of flowers was unpleasant. One day after the funeral, I lay on the couch in our living room and imagined that I heard eerie music, another after-effect of my first funeral experience.

During third grade, I missed about a third of school because I was sick so much of the time. The doctor prescribed a raw egg in milk once a day to give me strength. What a tasty medicine! Fortunately, I passed third grade, but I am not sure that I earned it.

Not all was gloomy in the new setting. In our back yard, we had a huge black cherry tree. We loved to play around it.

When the cherries got ripe, what joy we had gorging on the delicious fruit. Once I cried "Oh, I got stains on my clothes!" But my understanding and compassionate mother was very tolerant of the blue stains.

There was a large barn-like building behind the house. The first floor was used as a garage, but on the second floor, we played and pretended and roughhoused. On that floor, there was also a mysterious locked room, belonging to the owner of our house. We tried our best to look through cracks in the wall into that mysterious room for lost treasure but it was locked up tight and we could not see in.

We devised all sorts of frightening things for our homemade "funhouse." We made a low seesaw with a board that dropped down when the blindfolded victim walked over it. Scary things hung from the ceiling. We assembled anything else our imagination could conjure up. One day I led Bobby Eltringham through our fun house. The last item was a huge box. I told him, "Lift the lid off that box and see what is inside." My friend David Davies was inside dressed in a skeleton outfit. When Bobby lifted the lid and Dave jumped out yelling, the poor boy screamed and ran downstairs and home. We thought that was great fun.

David Davies and I became close friends that year, and our friendship continued through High School, even after we moved back down town. But Dave pulled a trick on me too. In our back yard, there was a tall wooden fence with one loose board we could push to get out of the yard. One day when I tried to get out, with my hands on the adjoining boards, I felt something sticky. Removing my hands I found them full of tar that Dave had put there as a booby trap. Such tricks continued through High School.

Another significant turn in the road came after Granddad died. Grandmother and our family purchased a home downtown on Walnut Street, one of the few level areas in Ashland. It was here I have the most vivid memories of a happy childhood. We enjoyed climbing the grape arbor in our backyard and eating luscious concord grapes. The ground and cement walk became littered with shells from those grapes, but we happily cleaned up after our feast.

At the rear of our small backyard, there was a garage and a storage building. Dad went to work at three o'clock in the afternoon, so after school we played in the garage, on the roof of the garage and in the small storage building we called our "playhouse." There was a six-foot space for a sidewalk between the garage and the playhouse. Since the garage roof was quite a bit higher than the playhouse roof, I enjoyed the thrill of jumping across that span from the garage roof to the playhouse roof. I am sure my mother never caught me doing that! God protects even reckless children.

I am still nostalgic as I think back to that happy time: playing "Kick the Can," "May I?" "Hot Tamale," baseball down by the dairy, Penny Ante for match sticks down by the huge weeping willow tree, throwing stones at bottles floating down the black creek (made black by the coal and sulfur that polluted the water). Almost daily, I would go to Pepper's back yard and call out, "Georgie, do you want to come out to play?" We also played checkers. One time, I crowned his checker and said, "I crown you king of the Jews!" George replied, "Do you know who you are talking about?" Was I ever embarrassed!

One day, as we were playing in the backyard, rocks began to fly over the fence from the back alley. I opened the large wooden gate and looked out to see two boys running away. Since the wooden gate to our five-foot high backyard fence hid me from view, when rocks began to fly into our yard again, I ran out of the yard and chased the boys down the street. I caught up with the bigger one and tackled him. I got him down and was on top of him when his brother ran home and got his father. The father came running and seeing the situation said, "I thought you said he was a big guy." He turned around and went back home without "rescuing" his son! I saw a father who was willing to let his son fight his own battles. It was during those years I too learned to fight my own battles.

Doris and I loved animals. Besides our dog Queenie, we had a cat and rabbits. We also picked up stray cats and dogs, but Dad always managed to make us get rid of them. We loved one dog in particular. We named him "Brownie." He was so affectionate and playful and we were able to keep him for some time, but, to our dismay, Dad finally decided to get rid of him without our knowing it. He took Brownie to work and dropped him off many miles from our home. We wondered what had happened to him until Dad explained that he had dropped him off, hoping that someone would take him in. Several days passed and Brownie showed up again. He had traveled, like Lassie, many miles and found his way home. Dad was still determined that he could not stay with us. So, he spoke to a man at his work who said, "Leave him with me,

I will get rid of him." We were so sorry and felt that the man had killed our Brownie.

Since we had a coal furnace in the cellar and a coal stove in the kitchen, my chores were to swing open the metal door of the furnace, dig my shovel into the pile of coal in the bin and feed that fiery dragon. Carrying the coal hopper from the damp, musty cellar and up the steep cellar stairs, I felt the strain on my growing muscles. In the kitchen, I opened the iron lid on the stove and shoveled in two scoops of those "black diamonds." Opening the metal swing door under the grate, I would shovel the dusty ashes into the coal bucket and carry it down into the cellar for disposal later. My sister, Doris, had the chore of gathering up the dirty dishes, washing them in the old enamel sink and drying them on the cotton towel which hung on a rack near the sink.

I spent time in that damp cellar making things on my lathe and would gather scraps of wood for my projects at a local lumberyard. I loved the smell of the wood and the experience of seeing things coming into shape. Proudly, I gave gifts formed from wood to family and relatives. The prize accomplishment in my early teens was a jewelry box shaped like a beehive with a removable tray inside. I even made an oak baseball bat.

During my senior year at school, I ventured into the task of making a little rowboat. Purchasing waterproof plywood, I set to work making a frame. When the frame was finished, I bent the plywood around the frame. After I caulked the boat and painted it blue trimmed in yellow, the project was almost complete, except for a name. I chose "Verna Mae" after my mother and painstakingly painted that name on the sides of my boat. The little boat provided many hours of fun rowing, fishing, swimming and drifting with the current.

I also liked to use my chemistry set in the basement. A mixture containing magnesium that photographers used to make a flash for their pictures fascinated me. One night, my nephew Craig and I took the mixture, wrapped it in paper, and set out on a mischievous mission. I dropped the package on the doorstep of a saloon, lit it and knocked on the door. I hid behind a tree to see the fun. But the paper went out and no one came to the door. I tried the second time and the flame went out again, but still no one opened the door. We tried the third time and someone opened the door just as the flash went off! We didn't wait to see the expression on his face. We went running like jackrabbits down the street before we could be caught.

I got a little camera and some darkroom equipment so I could take and develop my own pictures. It was intriguing to try trick photography and see the results show up in the darkroom. With the cameras of that time, it was possible to take double exposures. This provided the opportunity to make trick photos. I had my nephew, Craig, dress in my sister's bathing suit and face in one direction. I took his picture; then he dressed in his own suit and faced in the other direction. Taking the double exposure, the picture showed him facing himself, once as a girl and once as himself. Another double exposure, with Craig dressed in a sheet, gave the impression of a ghost against the fence.

As I grew older, football became my passion. Every day, after school, I headed across the black creek to a large field where neighborhood kids gathered to play. I enjoyed the rough and tumble, especially running the ball. I had learned to throw a tackler off my back with a twisting motion. My friend David learned how to shoelace tackle. I hated to be tackled from behind that way just as I was about to run for a touchdown!

In the summer, swimming and fishing took up a lot of my time. Mrs. Pepper, George's mother, often loaded her Packard with neighborhood kids and drove us six miles to Berry's dam. It was there I learned to dive and even dared to go off the thirty-foot high tower. I believe the Lord was teaching me to be willing to "step out in faith" because a prayer was on my heart when I took the dive. The Peppers were good friends. They owned a bottling factory and made Pepper's special Ginger ale, the best I ever tasted. It was famous all over that part of the state. George was my age and we spent much time together, playing in the alley, swimming, hiking up on the adjacent hills and boxing in his grandfather's garage. Doris was good friends with Jackie Pepper and his sister, Jeannie.

I guess I was considered an aggressive boxer, so when George's friends decided to hold boxing matches, I was paired off with Vince Cunningham. Apparently, Vince had been taught how to jab and box. I lit into him with arms flailing, but he jabbed and jabbed and won each of the three rounds. They did give me one round because he hit below the belt. My head hurt so much that I could not even watch the other matches but just lay down and suffered. So much for my boxing career! The Lord has his ways of showing us our limitations!

Dad worked six days a week, but he found time to take me fishing and taught me to shoot a twenty-two rifle. Our family went on a vacation every summer to the Loyalsock Creek in Lycoming County. How I looked forward all winter long to those two weeks of swimming, fishing, hiking and family fun. My family and the families of my two older sisters rented one or two cabins so we could spend our vacations together.

One evening our first summer there, the head of a deer appeared at our living room window, looking inquisitively at us and cocking his head as a puppy does. "Oh, look at that; he must be tame." "Look at those horns!" We were enthralled and excited. When the head disappeared, I sprang to the door – only to see the two Sausser boys running away with a mounted deer head! They were laughing at those gullible city folks. We also laughed at how naïve we were.

These same boys taught us many things about the Loyalsock Creek, including how to catch hellgrammites by turning over rocks and flushing them into a net. Then we removed the hooks on their tail so they could not cling to the rocks on the bottom of the stream. We hooked them through the collar and had the best bass bait around. The Saucers also showed us the secret path to the Seven Falls where we caught native brook trout.

We took my little rowboat, the Verna Mae, along on our vacation. One night, my nephew Craig and I went fishing in the boat in order to catch some large bass we had spotted in the daytime. We sat there a long time, patiently waiting for a bite. We were about to give up, when Craig hooked into a monster; it bent his rod and pulled so hard on his line that it escorted my little boat around the creek before he could land it. Excited, Craig handed the rod to me and said, "Here, feel how heavy it is!" When the tug on the line eased up, I tried to get my net under the catch. I couldn't get under it so I took hold of the line and attempted to pull the catch into the boat, but the higher I lifted the line, the more of that monster came up out of the water. Finally, standing up I managed to get it into the boat. It was a fat, four-foot long eel. It swam around in the water in my boat until I stabbed it with my fishing knife. Two excited kids ran barefoot, without noticing the rough stones, holding the heavy, long and slimy eel. When we arrived out of breath to the cabin with our prize we shouted out, "Look everyone what we caught!" Our amazed families gathered around and celebrated with us.

Every summer Craig and I spent time together. He lived several weeks at our home and I spent several weeks at his home at King Manor, near Norristown, PA.

These were times of fun and adventure. On the way back from swimming in Berry's Dam, we had to walk our bikes up a hill. Over the guardrail of the hill was a steep divide where trains passed through. As we walked up the hill, two large police dogs attacked us. "Run Craig!" I shouted and jumped over the guardrail, grabbed a tree limb and slid part way down the embankment where the dogs could not reach me. Craig did not know there was a divide there, thinking he was going to run onto a field, he jumped over the guardrail and tumbled straight down the steep cut in the road. It was so steep, I could not see him. Then I heard a train coming and I called frantically for him to run. In the excitement, I forgot all about the dogs, which by this time had their fun in scaring us and had left. Craig managed to run along the track and got out of the way before the train came. His only injury from the tumble down that embankment was a nasty cut on his leg.

I invited a neighborhood friend, Chester Ernst, to go with me to fish in a trout-filled reservoir high on a mountain above Gordon, a town about two miles from Ashland. I let him ride on the handlebars of my bike, but when we came to the steep, winding road that led up to the reservoir, I had to push the bike. It was about a mile to the top of the mountain. We fished for a while in that clear water where we could see many trout swimming around. As hard as we tried, we only succeeded in drowning worms, so we headed home. Riding home would be a lot easier because it was down hill all the way. However, with Chester on the bike with me, I had to brake hard all the way down the steep, winding road. Near the bottom, the road was straight and ended in a 'T' at a more traveled road. As I let the bike roll faster and faster, I joked with Chester, "The brakes don't work!" When we were at top speed, I thought I had better begin to brake—but, to my dismay, the brakes really didn't work! It felt as if we were catapulted forward! In spite of spragging my feet, we hurtled across the busy road and into the woods bumping along until a tree branch knocked Chester from the bike. I continued until my bike fell over, spilling me to the ground. There I lay, with smoke coming from the coaster brake of my prized bike. Pushing my bike, we walked the two miles to my home. Curious, I took the coaster brake apart to find it completely melted inside!

As I look back, I see that we kids did dangerous things I would never let my own children do. George Pepper and I thought it was always an adventure going up into the hills, but to get there we had to pass over large hills of black, discarded slate. Between two of these hills, fifty feet down, ran railroad tracks on a main line. Connecting the hills was a steel structure of I-beams that formed a trestle for some kind of use in past days. There was no floor and we had to hold on to the perpendicular and crisscrossed beams. We walked and crawled carefully on the I-beams beneath our feet until we, with bated breath, got to the other side. One slip would have led to severe injury or death. Sometimes a train came belching its black smoke up as us as we crossed over. Thankfully, that black cloud of sulfur and unburned coal did not overcome us! We also liked to climb the steep inclines, left over from strip mining, to search for sulfur diamonds. I still have a black coal-filled scar on my left knee from sliding down the stripping!

I was always willing to take a dare. One summer when I was with Craig in King Manor, his father, Jim, took us to a swimming pool. My uncle Jim was a cut-up. He took a dive into the shallow part of the pool. "Now it's your turn," he challenged us and dared Craig and me to do the same. I took the dare. I looked at the shallow water and wondered if I could duplicate his feat. I dived in and ended up with scrapes and scratches from head to toe!

One day I tried to be a hero, hoping to rescue the robins in the big trees near our house. Someone had yelled, "The blackbirds are killing the robins!" I saw what I thought was the culprit cringing in the corner of a patio. Therefore, with my trusty B-B gun, stealthily I crept up on the supposed culprit, took aim and shot it. "Got it!" I exclaimed. When I approached my victim, to my dismay, I discovered it was a baby bird! Actually, the blackbirds were all excited because one of their babies had fallen out of its nest. We had a funeral for my poor little victim. I felt just terrible. I hope I learned not to jump to conclusions.

Winters were as much fun as summers. Snowball battles, making snowmen and snow caves presented fun things to do on the long, cold, winter days. We went ice-skating at "Coney Island," a small lake about a mile out of town. I wasn't very good because my ankles seemed too weak. We also enjoyed skiing on small hills at the country club and on other hills surrounding Ashland. My skis were primitive, only about four feet long with single leather straps that fastened my feet in place. But I had great fun anyway.

Sledding was special. We rode our sleds down the steep street between Center and Walnut. I organized a "train" of sleds to descend the hill. Each rider clasped the feet of the rider in front of him and we started to sled down the hill. But a new boy in the neighborhood, Bobby Roebuck, wrecked the train by pulling the middle sled and caused everyone to tumble off their sled. He thought it was great fun, but we were not amused. I jumped up and warned him not to do that again. So, we tried a second time to sled down coupled to each other but he wrecked our train again! Angrily I jumped up with fists flying and lit into him. He fought back, and as usual when I was in a fistfight, I got a bloody nose. I don't how he made out. However, I think we were successful on the third try at having a train of sleds, without interference from Bobby.

Although the street we crossed was a less traveled alley, some of the streets that kids sledded on were dangerous. An acquaintance of mine sledded down a hill, onto busy Center Street. It was a steep hill and provided a thrilling ride. But it was dangerous since there was so much traffic. One day he glided under the wheels of a huge coal truck. He was killed instantly. Again, the tenuousness of life struck me as I thought of his mangled body.

JUNIOR HIGH SCHOOL

In sixth grade, I started taking lessons at school on the violin. I learned to play the tune to Twinkle, Twinkle little Star with the words: "I can play my violin, just as well as Steely (our teacher) kin." Unfortunately, I did not continue after a year. Junior high school filled me with apprehension, and when I missed my first violin practice there, I was too embarrassed to go to the next one. Dad could play the piano well and I could have taken lessons on the piano in our living room. But I did not even try to learn, because fun and sandlot football were more important to me. I still regret that I made the easier choice instead of the discipline of practice.

Seventh grade was another change in my zig-zag path and a threatening challenge. All the town's grade school children came together to one school perched high on a hill in Ashland. Everything was so different from the small classes in elementary school and I responded with less than a happy spirit.

The first day in class, I had my feet on the back of Emlin Whipple's chair. It apparently annoyed him and he told me to stop. I didn't and he said he would meet me outside after school. I told my friend David Davies that I was going to get into a fight. That day we waited in vain for Emlin. We waited several other nights, because, I thought my honor was on the line. Finally, I got him to agree to fight. We went farther along the hill, about a hundred yards from the school. I put a chip on my shoulder and when he knocked it off. I punched him. He seemed surprised and said, "Oh punching huh!" and we started to wrestle. As we struggled on the hilly ground, the principal spotted Emlin and called him back to the school. I headed for home as fast as I could run. The next morning, she said, "The boy who was fighting with Emlin Whipple must stay after assembly is dismissed." My heart sank and I feared I would face the belt that she purportedly had behind her lectern. Shaken, I came forward to receive my punishment. We were both sentenced to stay after school every day until Christmas time. Emlin and I became friends, as we served out our time! It was foolish of me to think that my honor was on the line when he challenged me. He probably had no real intention of fighting over that little incident.

Around our school was an eight-foot high fence with pronged wires at the top. There were two gates out of the schoolyard, but one day the gate I generally used was locked because I had stayed after school. To avoid the long way around the school, I shoved my books under the fence and climbed up and over that chain link barrier. I jumped down but my wrist caught on the three-pronged wires and ripped open a deep gash in the flesh of my thumb. I can thank the Lord that I did not hang there from the wrist because there was no one around that isolated spot. "What can I do now?" Thinking I might bleed to death there on Stormy Hill, filled me with dread and caused me to panic. With blood streaming from my hand, I ran down a long flight of concrete stairs to Walnut Street and then farther down the hill to Center Street, across Center Street and up to Dr. O'Neil's office. I banged frantically on his door, but there was no response. Not knowing what to do, I walked down the street with my hand held out, blood streaming from the wound. I remember a passerby looking and shaking his head.

Finally, Mrs. Stroemeyer, a high school teacher, saw my plight, rushed me into her sister's cloth shop, wrapped my hand in cloth and walked me several blocks to Dr. Spencer's office. There I was laid on a bed while the doctor worked on me. Mother arrived and, for the first time, my tears began to flow.

The next day, I faced the inquisition at school. The principal and several other people surrounded me, asking why I did not go to the other gate. In addition to a very sore hand, I felt humiliated. When the fourteen or so purple stitches were removed, my sister Doris watched. She almost fainted because she thought they were taking veins from my hand!

Coming home from school over the hill toward my house, I found an abandoned tire. It was great fun rolling that tire along the top of the hill. When I started down, I lost control of the tire and it went rolling faster and faster down hill. I tried frantically to catch up with it. Dismayed and frightened, I watched as it rolled toward Walnut Street and a row of houses. It rolled across the street, jumped a porch railing and banged into a swing. What was I to do? Should I run? I was so far away that I would never be recognized or caught. But that was not the honorable thing to do. So I faced the music and ran down to the red-faced man who was standing looking at the tire and seeing what damage it could have done. I confessed to him that the tire got out of control and that I was the source of the problem. Angrily he just said, "Get this tire out of here!" I obliged, relieved that he was not going to press charges!

Although I did well in grade school, changes seemed to come into my life in Junior High. I did not study as I should have and was willing just to get by. "Tough guys don't study." My teacher, Mrs. O'Neil, the sister of our family doctor, sensed that I was way behind my ability and often said, "Billy, you should be doing better."

I vaguely remember being in the Cub Scouts, but my Boy Scout experience is more vivid. We had a fun troop. I enjoyed the free-for-alls when the lights were turned out and we wrestled with anyone we could find. Indian style wrestling and cockfighting—trying to knock an opponent over while jumping on one leg—were great fun. I managed to earn enough badges for second class, but for some reason, I did not go further.

Mother sent us to Sunday School, where we collected red and blue Scripture cards for good attendance. When we had collected enough, we received a Bible. There I learned to sing, "Jesus Loves Me." When I was 14 years old, Doris and I were ready to join the Lutheran church. In order to join the church, it was necessary for us to attend catechism class for several months. We had to memorize long parts in preparation for the service during which we would join the church. The classes were not successful in leading me to trust Christ and Him alone for salvation. I did understand that Jesus died for the sins of the world, but I had not accepted Him as my personal Savior. I still thought God would weigh my good works against my bad to decide whether or not to let me enter Heaven. I was irritated having to attend those classes when I wanted to be out on the field across from the black creek, playing football.

After joining the church, I felt I no longer needed to go to Sunday School, so I stopped attending. Mother encouraged me to attend, but wisely did not force me. She was happy that I was at least attending church services regularly.

HIGH SCHOOL

In high school, my attitude toward studies remained the same. I was just willing to get by, get the assignments done and pass the tests. It wasn't until my senior year that the wasted opportunity to excel was revealed. We took an IQ test and I got one of the three highest scores in the school. Again, I was reprimanded for not doing better. I had never learned to study and excel to prepare myself for college.

Today it is difficult for me to understand what I was going through at this time. I became very girl-shy. I don't know why my high school graduation book described me as "Friendly, tall and good looking. What a smile! Not especially interested in girls." I was interested in girls, but could not bring myself to date in High School even though I had four sisters. The older three had been married, but Doris, two years younger than I, was very popular in High School. She taught me to dance, but I didn't go to dances during those years.

I was also frustrated because I could not play football. It was discovered that I had a "calcified chest." That meant that I had been exposed to tuberculosis and had some scarring in my lungs. Therefore, my father would not give me permission to play football. One class song was: "You gotta be a football hero to get along with the beautiful girls." Well, that left me out!

Nevertheless, in my sophomore year, I finally convinced my dad to sign for me to play football. I talked Dave into quitting the band and signing up for football too. How I enjoyed that first practice! I thought, "Finally, I get to play!" as I suited up for practice. The coach commended me on how I broke up a play and tackled the ball carrier. I had practiced for years on the sandlot so I guess I was pretty good. At least I thought so. However, as we were suiting up for practice the next day, the coach asked me to hang back to talk. He said the doctor's exam showed that I had an enlarged heart and I could not play. That was a terrible blow! Never since have I been diagnosed with an enlarged heart. I believe it was enlarged because I played so hard in sandlot football; many athletes have enlarged hearts. One of the greatest desires of my heart was to play my favorite sport on the high school squad. Now that opportunity was gone, so I went back to sandlot ball.

But that put me in another category in high school. Since I was not in the high school band, I seemed to be out of most things. I did join the Hi-Y, a Christian organization, but I don't remember much about it. I also joined the glee club and was even in the Junior play—in a non-speaking part that lasted about 30 seconds!

A foolish thing happened when I was a junior. I regret it to this day. As I passed by other students to catch up with Dave, someone punched me on the back. I turned around and punched back at the one I thought had hit me. Then Boogie Gressens, who was with this new kid in school said, "We'll wait for you outside." Now my honor was at stake, so instead of going home the back way as usual, Dave and I waited out front for him. We went into a nearby alley and put up our fists. I said, "Wait a minute, I need to take my jacket off." I had my jacket down over my arms when he rushed in and hit me in my face. I became so angry at this dirty trick that I tackled him and got him down. I felt like the victor until he did what was not in our "honor code"—no choking, scratching, or hitting when down. He reached up, caught me by the throat, and began choking me with strong wiry hands. I let him up and then an adult came and broke up the fight. I went home with the cut on my nose bleeding, not feeling sure of who had won.

The next day Boogie, the instigator, came up to me and asked me why I let him up. A few days later, I heard that the young man punched someone, who was sitting down with several other boys. He then ran away. I wondered if they were teasing him about our fight. He never showed up at school again. I still hope that I was not the cause. I have often wondered if he quit school altogether and where he ended up. I pray that foolish fight over nothing did not change the course of his life for the worse. I did not pick fights, but I felt I was honor-bound to respond when I was challenged.

In reality, I was a loner in high school, except for my friendship with David Davies. I continued to play sand lot football every chance I got and I enjoyed gym class. One day we were put in a sit-up competition. Everyone dropped out except another boy and me. We continued on and on. I dropped out first, but the next day, I could hardly stand up straight. Imagine how this self-conscious lad felt walking half bent over between classes!

Three nights a week, I set up pins at the Elks Club bowling alley. I still remember the dust as the balls hit the stuffed leather backup. There were two lanes, so I got to talk to the other pin boy to pass the time. I would pick up the balls, put them on the rack to send them back, then stoop over and pick up the pins and put them on retractable pins in the floor. Then I jumped up above the leather bag that absorbed the force of the bowling ball as it hit, causing dust to fly. It was good exercise and I earned a little money, most of which I spent on movies. Because we were sweaty, thirsty and tired, the bowlers brought 7-UP from time to time for us to drink. I drank it in spite of the beer and soap residue taste from those glasses that were merely rinsed.

Another blow to my expectations came when, at sixteen, I took my driver's test. I did not pass the eye exam. I needed glasses and that was a great disappointment to me. I had been dreaming of being a fighter pilot in the air force during the war, but the doctor said that was impossible since I would now be wearing glasses.

During the war, we had blackouts in Ashland in case of an air raid. I became a Civilian Defense messenger. When the sirens rang, excitement began. I wrapped my messenger band around my arm, got my flashlight, put red cellophane in front of the lens and ran out the door. It was eerie with all the lights of town turned out. I could almost feel the blackness of such nights. As long as the blackout lasted, I stayed at my post in front of the sewing factory and carried messages from one place to another. It was exciting to run through that pitch-black town with a flashlight covered with red-colored cellophane so enemy planes could not see us. "All clear" was proclaimed when the shrill siren sounded again.

Although my sister taught me how to dance, I didn't dance with anyone else. I went to some of the high school dances where my friend David Davies was a drummer. As much as I wanted to, I never dared to ask a girl to dance. However, when senior prom time came, I felt I had to make the break. I asked one of Doris' friends, Kitty Baglin, to the prom. But a frightening surprise awaited me when I got to the prom. I learned that we were to fill our cards with the names of others than our date. Cautiously, with card in hand, I approached several of the less threatening girls to fill my program. So, as girl shy as I was, I had to dance with a number of different girls. I was stiff, nervous and sweating, and hoped that my dance partner did not notice. The prom was not a pleasant affair for me!

JESUS BECOMES PERSONAL

One summer, when Doris and I were visiting my oldest sister, Harvena, she was bubbling over with what had happened to her and to Ruth—they had both come to trust Jesus as their personal Savior. Harvena had just spent a week at Keswick Grove, a Christian camp, and when she returned she was excited about the new things she had learned. Doris and I were extremely interested in her experience. We sat up, enthralled, until the wee hours of the morning listening to these new insights. I really hungered and thirsted for the things she had to say. It was the first time I heard about personally accepting Christ, and it is from that time that I date my personal acceptance of His death on the cross for my sins, not just the sins of the world in general. I realized that good works were the result of knowing Christ, and not the way to win my way to Heaven.

CHAPTER 2

ON THE WAY TO COLLEGE

In my senior year of high school I became interested in one particular subject—chemistry. I began to think about going to college to become a chemical engineer. However, when I graduated, I lacked geometry for entrance into Penn State. For several months I went back to high school to make up that subject. I also tried to get a job, but there were none to be had in the depressed coal region.

Another turn in my road was led of the Lord. There was work to be found around Philadelphia, and my sister, Ruth, invited me to stay with her family while I looked for a job. I enrolled in evening classes in Philadelphia at Lincoln Prep and commuted from Rebel Hill in Conshohocken several times a week.

Coming home in the pitch-black night, I had to pass through a cemetery behind our house. At first, I hurried through the cemetery, alertly keeping my eyes on the gravestones that rose from the ground like threatening shadows. But, after a few scary nights, I became accustomed to walking among the gravestones without looking for something abnormal!

I found work first at a box factory for $.50 an hour; then at a chemical plant for $.55 an hour and finally found a good paying job at $1.29 an hour at Keasbey and Mattison, an asbestos plant in Ambler, PA. It was good physical work but dusty with asbestos. Fortunately, I was not a smoker and, except for slight scarring, I think little damage was done to my lungs.

Half way through the year, the bulletin board advertised for a lathe operator. I had a wood lathe in our home, so I applied, stating only that I knew how to run a lathe. I got the job! I learned quickly and was turning out a good number of cement and asbestos couplings on a large metal lathe.

A few days after I started, one of the workers, a union man, told me not to make more than a certain quantity. We worked swing shift, so with no foreman on the night shift, I could do my quota in two hours! A time-control man watched us work and checked out our machine and movements and finally, we were told we would go on piece work—just what the union man wanted. With piece work, I was making much better money, but after a week, the three shifts had backlogged so many couplings that they laid off one shift and I was transferred to another labor job, working with a crane operator to lift and stack huge cement pipes. So much for unions!

That year with Ruth and Clayton and their children was a year of maturing and spiritual growth for me. I gained confidence, though I was still girl-shy. Bowling every week, swimming at the dam near where we lived, fishing, and enjoying life helped make that an unforgettable year. We went to Abrams Chapel, a little Independent Baptist Church, where I learned much about the Bible and grew in the Lord under Pastor Robby Robin's ministry. It was a year of growth in the knowledge of the things of the Lord and His Word—but my goal in going to college was still to gain position, fame and security. I dreamed of the day I would be a well-known scientist, comfortably settled in a luxurious home with several cars.

I hitchhiked to get home to my family in Ashland, about four hours from Conshohocken. I was saving money to buy a car, but one weekend Dad asked me to look in the garage. He had bought a car and told me I could pay the $400 for it as I earned money at my job. It was a thirty-seven Plymouth, twelve years old with a noisy motor. I painted it a dark blue with powder puffs, a painting fad at the time. I also redid the torn fabric on the inside of the roof with a light blue vinyl. I thought I had the best car around even though it burned as much oil as gas!

While working at the laboring job, I became good friends with Nels Nelson, a rugged football player. He and I had fun wrestling at odd moments on the job. When he had to go to Virginia to try out for the Virginia Tech football team, I offered to take him in my "new" car. He got in my car, along with another rugged heavyweight who also wanted to get on the Tech team. We headed south, expecting a long trip, but we got only about twenty miles along when the car stopped dead. We three strong young men tried to push it off the road, but it would not budge. The two left me sitting alone in Downingtown, Pennsylvania. I didn't know what to do. They continued on by hitchhiking and I had my prize car towed into a garage. It had a frozen bearing and it would cost hundreds of dollars to rebuild the engine. My savings soon were gone. I worried, "Now how am I going to pay my dad for the car?"

After that eventful year, I was in for the surprise of my life! The Lord began to direct my path in a way I had not expected. He showed me that I needed discipline and humility. I enrolled in the Penn State extension campus in Pottsville, Pennsylvania, located about sixteen miles from Ashland. Since I liked and did well in chemistry in high school, I started to major in Chemical Engineering. I was overconfident of my ability to do well. In high school, studies had come easily for me—I never had to take books home. Mother was apprehensive about my grades month after month, but I always managed to bring home average grades, just enough to keep her satisfied. New students at Penn State had to start in an off campus center, and Pottsville was the closest to home. Instead of renting a room in Pottsville, I lived at home and commuted. Living at home was difficult when it came to studies because I had never learned to study in high school and I was easily distracted at home. Bull sessions at school and fellowship evenings stole away precious study time. I was also overconfident about my ability to understand what was taught in class. Consequently, I did not do the Chemistry homework of ten equations to work out each day, even when they became mathematically complex. Our semester grade depended entirely on our final exam. As the exam time approached, I desperately studied to cram an entire semester's work into one week. I failed the chemistry exam by two points and did poorly in math and physics, subjects essential to chemical engineers. I guess I fooled my self in thinking I could get by as I did in high school. With one F and several Ds, my hopes of breezing through college soon faded. Learning how to study was no easy task for me and self-discipline was extremely difficult. Consequently, my grades for all four semesters at the Penn State Center were very poor.

We had Reserve Officers Training as a requirement and I was appointed second in command, First Lieutenant. We were instructed to give out demerits to the cadets whose dress was sloppy. A demerit meant one hour of work and the need to stay at school, even for the commuters. Instead of giving a demerit, I spoke privately to men to correct their demeanor. Other officers stood secretly watching in order to give out demerits. Towards the end of the second semester, I was told that there were too many officers and they had observed my scuffed shoes after my drive from Ashland, so I was demoted to First Sergeant. I think the real reason might be that I was not tough enough on the cadets! It was a humiliating experience. The Lord knew I had to become more humble. He was providing a life experience in humility.

By this time, my shyness with girls had subsided somewhat and I attended formal dances with Mary Ellen Boyer, a close friend of my sister, but I still did not have a girlfriend. I was far from a womanizer, but I was looking for the girl of my dreams.

In the summer of 1950, our family went to Canada to a resort on Lake Cashagawiggamog. Doris and I played tennis and vainly tried golfing. We had a pretty waitress, Joan Walker, who provided us with a cultural laugh. I asked if I could have a soda and noted a questioning look in her eyes. But she went to the kitchen and came back with a box of baking soda! Their name for soda was "pop." I was impressed with Joan and we got acquainted, swimming and at a dance. This was the first time that I was infatuated with a girl. I hated to leave that resort, but we promised each other that we would write. We did for a time, but that didn't last more than a year.

A DECISION THAT CHANGED MY LIFE

Another turning point came towards the end of summer when I had a distressing decision to make. It was time for me to continue at the main campus in State College. I was strongly tempted to quit when I found myself on probation. At the end of my own resources and not knowing what course to take, I was thrown on the Lord for an answer. Again I thought, "Trust in the Lord with all your heart, lean not to your own understanding, in all your ways acknowledge Him and He will direct your path." I drove up to Penn State a month before school was to start. I vividly remember the two and a half hour trip, praying fervently that the Lord would open the way and show me His will. And He did!

I shall never forget that summer afternoon. After having been directed to several people, I found myself in the office of the Dean of the School of Chemistry and Physics. I spoke to him about transferring to a straight Chemistry course with the hopes of teaching in high school. I found, however, that when one is on probation, it is difficult to move from one "school" to another, even on the same campus. I would have to raise my grades in Chemical Engineering to transfer to his department of Chemistry. In the course of conversation, I mentioned that I had heard in a lecture of the wide open opportunities in the field of Ceramics or Ceramic Engineering, closely allied with Chemical Engineering but dealing more specifically with the chemistry and engineering of nonmetallic, heat treated earth materials—glass, refractories, and later semi-conductors and transistors. He offered to arrange an interview with Dr. Henry, Dean of the School of Mineral Industries. After a short talk, Dr. Henry decided to take a chance on me. My trip to Penn State was filled with desperate prayer, but my trip home was filled with thanksgiving and praise for the working of the Lord as He directed my path. Away from home at Penn State campus, I flourished. I took a non-credit course on "how to study" and another in typing. My grades shot up to A's and B's the first semester. I found Ceramics extremely interesting and practical. This was a turning point in my college life as I experienced this dramatic answer to prayer.

I attended InterVarsity Christian Fellowship meetings on the fourth floor of Old Main every week and tried the Lutheran Students Fellowship. Not taking the initiative in making friends at those meetings, I just went to InterVarsity for the spiritual food. It seemed that no one tried to befriend me. Since then, I learned the truth of a little saying: "I went out to find a friend and I did not find one. Then I went out to be a friend and they were everywhere." However, I did want others to know about the deeper experience I was having with the Lord, and I told my friends about the plan of salvation, when the time was appropriate. One student in particular, an admitted atheist, burdened my heart. He was moral and clean living, but he did not believe that any God existed. I sowed the seed whenever I could, but to my knowledge, he never accepted the Lord.

Except for one blind date, I did not date at all for the next two years. For sports, I spent time in Intramural football and basketball. One time at the gym, I was talking with a fellow who was on the wrestling team. For fun, I tackled him and pinned him! Then he challenged me and this time he pinned me!

Because of a football accident, I had a trick knee, which frequently went out of joint causing pain. It normally went back into place. But playing basketball one day, my knee locked up and did not correct itself. I was hardly able to walk and went to the infirmary. From there, I was sent to the Penn State athletic trainer, who worked on me to get it in place. The pain he caused was excruciating. After trying on three separate occasions, he gave up and said I needed an operation. Since it was close to the Easter holiday, I had the operation at Geisinger Hospital in Danville without missing school.

Some of the dorms were old Navy barracks. The closeness in this kind of living gave me an opportunity to make some good friends, so it was not all study. The first night there, I was awakened by what sounded like shooting in our hall. I dived under my bed, only to discover that someone had set off firecrackers in the hall! We horsed around and had a good time kidding each other and competing in ping-pong and other pastimes. I set my electric alarm clock every Saturday night so I could get up to go to chapel.

One Saturday night, I arose to go to the bathroom and I heard a commotion in the hall. I tried to turn on the lights, but they would not go on. Then I saw a figure in the dark jumping into a phone booth. I knew he was up to no good, and I knew that alarm clocks had to have electricity to get the guys up for church. I swung the door open and said, "You had better stop this or someone is going to get hurt." "Are you going to do it?" he challenged, "If you want to fight, I'm ready, but the lights must go on first." So, he and his buddy turned the main switch on. I went to get a bandage for my leg because I had recently had the operation to remove cartilage from my knee. We squared off with fists high, and then he said, "Look, you don't want to fight and neither do I. Let's forget about it." "OK," I said, "but the light must stay on. People want to hear their alarm clocks to get up for church." As they left, his friend, said, "We'll be back!" But they never came back. Maybe they heard how well I did in a sport-boxing match with one of the guys in our dorm. In fact, another guy in the dorm was on the boxing team and hearing of our little match, he said he wanted to box with me. That never happened, and I am glad. I would have been no match for someone trained in boxing. Unfortunately, he did not return to school after the summer and I later learned that he had drowned.

Every summer I managed to get a job. One summer I enlisted with other fellows from the coal region to work on the railroad between Coatesville and Philadelphia, PA. We lived in barracks and were trucked to our work every day. Our job was to shovel gravel between the tracks. It was hot and hard work. On my first day, a machine came after us tamping down the gravel we were shoveling. It might have been an initiation or something, but I was left on one side of the tracks trying to keep ahead of the relentless machine while two men were on the other side. What a job! Every hour they came around with salt tablets and water to prevent us from fainting in the heat. They fed us great, protein rich meals and every night I fell exhausted into my upper bunk bed. It was a dangerous job because it was on an express-line and the trains came so fast and frequently around a blind curve. After I went back to school, I learned that a train killed one of the members of the crew I had been on. I had managed to save $100 that summer which I gave to Doris for her schooling at Philadelphia School of the Bible. My grandmother was paying my tuition at Penn State, but Doris was not getting any financial help. Too often at that time, the feeling was that a boy needed a college education as the breadwinner, but girls didn't need it in the same way. Thankfully, things have changed!

Chapter 3

In the summer before my senior year, I got a job as a lab assistant in a research lab at International Resistance Company in Philadelphia. I rented a room at the Philadelphia School of the Bible and walked to work every day. We worked under the supervision of a professor from the University of Iowa. Little did I realize that another college student and I were working on a project that would have a revolutionary impact on electronics. We connected wires to small ceramic discs and passed electricity through them. Ceramic normally is an insulator, so to see electricity pass through the disc was amazing. Then the disc, when immersed, provided enough resistance to boil the water. These experiments and others like them led to the development of transistors and semiconductors. We did the experiments without realizing the potential of what we were doing.

In the evenings, I spent my time either at the library listening to Stephen Foster records or at Leary's Bookstore where thousands of books were on sale. The Bibles and other

Christian literature especially fascinated me. I bought Bibles for all of my family members. I believe the Lord was just then beginning a work in me. He was calling me into the ministry He had for me, instead of glass research. I admired my sister, Doris, who was engaged to Larry Puckett. After graduation they intended to marry and go to Mexico as missionaries. Their willingness to spend their lives in the Lord's service made a deep impression on me.

My personal faith in the Lord was growing at this time. I wrote the following:

As my busy mind turns to thoughts of Thee,
The tensions of the day cease to be.

Like the peaceful calm of a glassy pool,
Thy presence stills the heart of this fool.

When the blackest night seems to loom ahead;
When the path still unseen causes dread,

How my life is robbed of the victory
Of the peace Thy pure Word promised me.

When to live is Christ and to die is gain,
Thoughts of fear and worry are all vain.

For my life's been hid, oh my Christ, with Thee,
Since that day I saw Thee on the tree.

Like a baby hid in his father's arm,
I am kept by Thy love, safe from harm.

On Thy map of time my future is planned.
Thou dost hold each detail in Thy hand.

Oh the joy of rest in this blessed word!
The response of my love has been stirred.

But it's not enough to recline in Thee,
For Thy Word has promised work for me.

A faith without works is revealed to be,
Dead as death and of no use to Thee.

Faith issues in works and proves itself true
As it prays, believes and seeks to do.

When my busy mind turns to thoughts of Thee,
And I feel the sweet rest calming me

Oh let me not fall into a dead sleep
Let me rise, be useful, Thy charge keep.

During the first months of my senior year, a student in our dorm invited me to go with him to the Methodist Wesley Foundation for a square dance. At a large assembly hall, the leader told us to form two circles, boys in one and girls in the other. He played music and said, "When I stop playing, pair off with the girl next to you." When the music stopped, a pretty girl was between me and another boy. I crowded over and she became my partner. She seemed like a lovely girl and I found out she was the preacher's daughter. After the evening was over, I decided to ask her for a date, but I forgot her name! With a little bit of sleuthing, I found out and called Jane on the phone to ask her to go to a dance. She agreed. During the dance, I asked her what she was hoping to do after graduation. She said, "Be a missionary." Surprised, since I did not expect to meet someone at Penn State with that desire, I foolishly blurted out "a Christian missionary?" She replied sarcastically, "No, a Hindu missionary." At that time I wondered if she told guys that she wanted to be a missionary as a put off or so that they would treat her appropriately. However, since the Lord had begun working in my life and I was asking how could I best use my life, it got me to thinking.

Later she agreed to go to the Junior Prom with me. Because the prom was some time in the future, I had opportunity to see her at the Wesley Foundation a number of times and our friendship grew. On one occasion, she asked me what I thought about a proposal that a fraternity had made—to sponsor her as a candidate for Junior Class and Homecoming Queen. I said, "Sounds great. You'll surely win!" She became a candidate and asked me to accompany her. The prom was supposed to be semi-formal and I thought the men had a choice to wear a suit or a tuxedo. It was too late for me to rent a tuxedo in town, as there were none available, so I decided to wear my suit. I bought her a corsage to match her evening gown and drove to her home. There, her sister, Jody, and a friend, Rose Mary, were with their dates, Bill Tucker and Barry Montgomery. But the guys had tuxedos on! I had goofed. This was the first semi-formal dance I had attended on campus and did not know that was what the guys wore. I never did find out what "semi" meant on campus. Here I was, an odd-ball in a dress suit, taking a candidate for Junior Prom Queen to the dance! I didn't mind so much feeling like a country boy in a high-formal city setting, but I hated the thought of embarrassing her. But she did not say anything.

We had danced several dances when the time came for the master of ceremonies to announce the Junior Prom Queen. All the candidates held their breath. People waited expectantly. When the winner was announced, it was Jane Montgomery! She was voted Prom Queen and Homecoming Queen. They called her up on stage and crowned her Queen of the ball—Queen of the Junior class! Her privilege was to start the dance. But it was with a guy wearing a regular dress suit! She never complained.

At the Wesley Foundation, there was a couple also headed for missionary work. I began to examine my motives for life. Up until that time I dreamed about being in research and inventing some new, revolutionary glass product. I dreamed of having a home by a stream, like the Loyalsock Creek, having at least two cars and acquiring wealth. Now, my sister was going to be a missionary and several others whom I had met. I began to struggle with the thought that maybe that was what the Lord wanted for me.

Shortly before Christmas, I began to feel a burden for those of other lands who had never heard the Gospel. God began speaking to my heart, but I was far from willing to respond. As I read the Scripture and prayed, the conviction grew deeper. I attempted to rationalize away this strange feeling by telling myself that it was just a passing fancy. In prayer I argued with the Inner Voice by saying that I did not have the makings of a preacher or missionary. I hated to speak publicly. My only experience in a required speech course was painful and I squeaked out a C grade. How could I be a missionary and not be good at public speaking? And I was about to graduate in a career that I liked. The preceding summer, I enjoyed the job I had at the International Resistance Company. It was rewarding working in a research laboratory, conducting experiments on what was to become a revolution in ceramics and electronics, the groundwork for ceramic resisters and semi-conductors. While there I had the opportunity to witness to the other assistant—"Wouldn't I be more useful to the Lord as a Christian in industry?"

However, the conviction grew and I struggled with it every night for about two weeks. More doubts came. "Everyone expects me to pursue the career that I was headed for and I and was getting excellent grades. Am I not better suited for research? Besides, how could I change now that I am about to graduate?" I struggled for several weeks. Then at an InterVarsity Christian Fellowship meeting, the speaker showed an inspiring film, "The Flower of Tibet", and told of how the Lord had called him to be a missionary when he had prepared for another career. His message seemed directed just at me. I was convinced that I could fight no longer and I gave in to the Lord. That night, on the fourth floor of Old Main, I said,

"Lord, I am willing to go if that is what You want." A burden lifted from my shoulders and I began to have peace. Then on Sunday morning, as if the Lord was setting a seal on the call, a Methodist chaplain at the church gave an almost identical testimony of the Lord's calling him during his last year of college from an unrelated field into the ministry. Coincidence? I knew, and have known, from that moment that the Lord wanted me to serve Him in spite of my frailties and lack of ability. I could see how the Lord had been preparing me from the previous summer for that crucial moment. I reasoned that I could teach natives how to make bricks, another ceramic product, and speak one on one about the Lord.

Now the question was, where should I prepare? I spoke with the pastor, Dr. Frank Montgomery, who was of great encouragement to me. He gave me the address of four Methodist Seminaries. I also went to Philadelphia Bible Institute to visit Doris and to look that school over. They were having a revival at the school and emotions were very high. Having been in science and influenced by logical decisions, I reacted against the emotion I sensed, students weeping and confessing their sins. (Of course, later on I encouraged revival myself.)

I waited expectantly for an answer from the four seminaries to which I had applied. The first school that answered my application was Drew Theological Seminary in Madison, New Jersey. I took that as the Lord's choice for me and applied. I was accepted on the condition that I take a Philosophy course to make up for my lack of college preparation for seminary.

I completed my major in Ceramics, and just before graduation, several tempting offers came to me. Not having any money to pay for tuition at Drew, I wondered where I was going to get the money. I was interviewed for possible positions in Ceramics by RCA and by Sylvania. RCA offered me a full salary to travel for two years from plant to plant to learn the industry. Sylvania made the same offer but for one year. Maybe this was the way the Lord was going to provide! I began to "lean to my own understanding," but as I prayed, I realized that this would be unfair to those companies who would be investing in me in order that they could use me in some capacity in the future. Was Satan making one more attempt to get me back into thinking of fulfilling my earlier dreams of becoming a well-known scientist with financial security and the "good life?" I decided to take the step of faith, believing that somehow the Lord would provide. My Ceramics professor could not understand why I would give up a promising career to become a missionary. He probably thought the years of his teaching me were going to waste.

My friendship with Jane Montgomery had grown that year. In some ways, I felt like a big brother, but I also felt I loved her. She seemed sensitive to the needs of others and was concerned about why God would allow so much suffering in the world if He is a good God. I asked to meet with her and explained the plan of salvation using the bridge diagram. I also wrote a long letter trying to explain why, as a pastor's daughter, she might be experiencing these doubts. But I greatly admired her tender heart for suffering people.

At the Wesley Foundation, we were considered friends and did things together. I enjoyed square dancing with her as my partner. I used my car to take Jane, Jody and other Wesley friends to a retreat. We had fun marching around, playing improvised baseball and just acting up. After dinner we had a fine message. During the question and answer time, Jane stood and asked, "How can you tell if you are in love?" I thought, "She cannot be thinking of our relationship because we are just friends. She must have a boyfriend somewhere." Later, as we sat around a campfire, we sang a camp song that ended "that's how I love you." Jane turned to me and said, "I don't like that song."

Sometimes, I used my car to take a group of Wesleyites to churches in the district to represent the Wesley Foundation, supported by gifts from the churches. We told about how the ministry was a "home away from home."

As a "big brother," I walked her home from her late night debating club so she would not have to go through the dark campus. Of course, this was a treat for me and it was a good excuse to be with her too! But there was always a sense that she might not think of me as anything more than a friend. I wondered about a mysterious "friend" who showed up from time to time. Was she committed to him? Some things she said encouraged me. For instance, on one occasion she said that she and her sister, Jody, thought I might be a strict father (why did they discuss my qualities as a father?) and she spoke admiringly about my faith. There was a close friendship but no romance. Up to that time, I had never really kissed any girl, but I had thoughts of our friendship developing into love on her part. I am sure she knew how I felt, though I had not said anything.

Jane's sister, Jody, was more outgoing and fun loving than Jane. Once, when a Wesley group was going somewhere in a car, reserved Jane had to sit on shy Bill's lap. Jody exclaimed: "I want to see this!"

At the end of the school year we went to a conference in north central New York called "Casowasco." After dinner, Jane wanted to talk with me alone. We stood under a tree in the dark. Jane used that old cliché: "Let's just be friends, nothing more." By that I understood that she knew how I felt by my actions, not by my words. I had not verbalized my feelings for fear of losing her friendship. I agreed that we would be good friends. After we got back to Penn State, I said, "Goodbye Jane, I will miss you." And she replied, "I'll miss you too."

However, she did want to carry on correspondence when I was in seminary and always signed her letter, "Love, Jane." There were other incidents that seemed encouraging to me. I looked for any sign or hint that Jane was becoming more serious. She sent me an 8x10 full-length color photo of her as the Penn State May Queen and the current "Wesley Way," the annual booklet about life at Wesley. In retrospect, I can see God's hand in the whole thing. He had my true love waiting in the future. Nevertheless, it was a step on the way to deciding the kind of girl I wanted to marry: one with sensitivity for people and a heart to serve.

The summer after graduation, I drove an ice cream truck through different towns in the coal region around Ashland. I enjoyed ringing the bell and seeing the children run excitedly up to my truck for their treat of the day. Later, I got a temporary job on the Reading Railroad for a couple of weeks taking care of a small hotel where railroad engineers could spend the night before returning on their run. I lived at home in Ashland and commuted to Tamaqua, about an hour away.

One day the Lord forced my hand at preaching. The pastor of the Methodist Church in Ashland called saying he had heard that I was going to seminary. "Would you preach for me for two weeks while I am on vacation?" My heart raced. I thought, "How can I preach with no experience?" Again, I began to lean to my own understanding. "I must pray about it," I replied. A few days later, I visited him. In the course of our conversation, he said something like: "Some people say Jesus is divine. But I believe He walked on the line between divinity and humanity; and we can all do that!" The challenge was before me! If this is what the people in the church were hearing, I must preach! "OK, I will stand in for you," I told him.

On that hour drive to Tamaqua, I practiced and practiced my sermon on First Corinthians 13, emphasizing the love that Christ has for us. Then on Sunday morning, I stood behind the pulpit to lead a service in a church where I had never worshipped. My knees shook and my voice quivered as I went through the order of service and the Methodist ritual. Then it came time to preach. I prayed with all my heart asking the Lord to work through me. When, I stood up to preach, I looked at the people and thought about how they needed the Gospel—all fear was gone! I took my eyes off myself and allowed the Lord to speak through me. I enjoyed preaching that first sermon and could not wait until the next week. The

Lord had done a work in my heart when I experienced two necessary things in preaching: get your eyes off yourself and think about the needs of the people who sit listening. From that time on, I have enjoyed preaching and teaching. It was His grace and still is His grace.

SEMINARY

a new challenge

Seminary was a new challenge. I thought that Drew was not an evangelical school, but I needed that training to go out as a Methodist missionary. I appreciated John Wesley's Aldersgate experience and loved Charles Wesley's doctrinal hymns. I was pleased to see a statue on campus of Frances Asbury, itinerant missionary and first bishop of the Methodist church in America. But I came to Drew with the feeling that I would encounter liberalism full force and worried about the possibility of not finding fulfilling Christian fellowship.

At our first fellowship meeting, I spoke to several of my classmates about the Lord. I felt that I needed to witness to them. To my delight, I found out that they were evangelical Christians. We formed a group on campus that was known as the "fundies" for Fundamentalists. We did believe in the fundamentals of the Gospel, but I preferred the designation "Evangelical," because "Fundamentalist" was getting to be synonymous with legalism and separatism. We decided to form a prayer band, so I went around every night and gathered the men for prayer. On Wednesday nights, students met in the chapel for a good old-fashioned prayer and praise service. We had students from Asbury Theological Seminary, a more evangelical, non-denominational school in the Wesleyan tradition, where some Methodists prepared for the ministry. In order to be accredited, they came to Drew to finish their studies. This added to our group of evangelical students.

Most of my teachers were of the Neo-Orthodox school. The emphasis was "do not throw out the baby with the bathwater." Their approach was to attempt to "demythologize" the Bible. I believed literally in the Virgin birth of Jesus and His bodily resurrection. Yet, I learned much from them and from my period of study at Drew.

Those were profitable years because I had to evaluate and reevaluate my faith and what I considered the fundamental Gospel in the light of new ideas and approaches. It was necessary for me to sift and strain everything that came from the classroom lectern. Later I realized that this background in Neo-Orthodoxy, which came out of Europe, would be helpful in encountering differing approaches to the Bible. This was especially true as I served with the Greater Europe Mission and even when confronted with Pentecostalism, which had some of the same subjective elements. The Neo—Orthodox interpretation of the Bible was subjective: 'the Bible in print is not literally the Word of God, but it becomes the Word of God when it speaks to you.' However, I believed in the literal, historical, grammatical interpretation of the Bible, which was itself, the Word of God.

Because I had not studied Philosophy at Penn State, I was required to take an overview course where I was to learn about many philosophies and philosophers. It was a nightmare to cover so much in a one-credit course. What many students spent years studying were crammed into that one course. But I managed to pass it.

Though I enjoyed my classes, I reacted against some of the teaching, and was told to "loosen up." When I wrote in a paper for my New Testament professor, I said that I believed that baptism by immersion was the early Christian method and that I felt it was the right way to baptize. He acknowledged that he often had questioned infant baptism himself. (I later discovered that he was a graduate of Dallas Theological Seminary.)

When I graduated, my hymnology and homiletics professor, Dr. Haas, came up to me and said, "We knew where you stood theologically, but we respected your stand and your attitude."

On one occasion, God touched my heart in a special way over a small incident. My roommate, Bob, and I were headed to the chapel for a prayer meeting, but another friend was far behind, so I told Bob "Let's wait for him." After he caught up and we were walking together, I stopped to say a word to another friend. But they walked on and left me. I was touchy and angry at the slight. Then I went to the chapel, sat alone, and sang with the others "See from His head, His hands, His feet, sorrow and love flow mingled down. Did ee'r such love and sorrow meet or thorns compose so rich a crown?" That struck my heart and showed me how ridiculous my anger was, and how it sorrows Him, even while His love pours down on me. Tears flowed as I confessed my self-centeredness and thanked Him for His forgiveness.

Because of my interest in missions, I was made Friendship Committee Chairman. My task was to see to the comfort and well being of the foreign students who often felt so strange in this new land. I arranged it so that the foreign students had a place to go on holidays. I formed good friendships with Jose´ Valencia, whose father was a bishop in the Philippines, Varghese from southern India, Vincent Adams from the Virgin Islands and others. I often had one of them in my parent's home over the holidays. Other close friends included Bob Carruthers, Paschal Jackson, Harold Himes, Ron Lindow and Harold Johnson.

The Lord made possible other privileges: being a reporter on the *Circuit Rider* campus newspaper, serving as Senior Class Treasurer and ushering for the daily chapel worship.

MINISTRY

a new experience

Another step of faith came the first year at Drew when I became Assistant Pastor in charge of youth at the Woodbridge, New Jersey, Methodist Church. I had never been involved with a youth group, so I was thrown on the Lord to help me lead and love those rambunctious teens. The salary solved my financial need and provided me with a good opportunity to minister while in school. Rev. William Justice, the pastor, patiently taught me many practical things about the ministry.

The young people were a challenge. Rowdy and hard to handle they were, but just as likable as they were rowdy. I remember asking the young people to write: "Why I think I am a Christian." I got all kinds of answers: "My family is Christian," "I go to church" and "I try to be good." Only one answered, "Because I believe in Jesus as my Savior." I knew that I had my work cut out for me. During that year, Shirley Kennedy, a member of the church who did secretarial work for the pastor, came to the meetings to play the piano and to assist with the youth. The young people liked to tease us as if we were romantically interested in each other. However, I had no such thoughts. I considered her a friend and a co-worker, and besides, Jane was still on my mind.

One weekend we took the young people to Keswick, NJ to a youth conference. At one meeting, a number of the kids from other churches got up and gave a testimony of how they had come to know Christ as a personal Savior. Our young people had never given a testimony. It was something new and surprising to them. That led many of them to examine their own spiritual life and several made the decision to accept Christ personally. Some of the kids did not respond and the group became divided between the saved kids and the others. The seed was sown and my hope is that they came to know Christ later on.

That year I assisted in the worship services and was able to preach at a morning service. The Pastor and his wife were very helpful and encouraging. As a going away present, they gave me a large book of poetry called Masterpieces of Religious Verse, which I have used many times in my sermons.

Jane and I continued to correspond during my first year at Drew Seminary. The following summer, I had my last date with her. We went swimming at Black Moshannon Lake and later ate dinner with her family. I helped clean up by drying the dishes. The Montgomerys made me feel right at home. Jane played a piece on the piano for me and afterwards, we went to a movie.

When I walked her home, she invited me in. We sat on a little bench inside the front door and conversed for several hours. She told me of her coming missionary endeavor in California at a young women's home for disturbed youth and I told her about my new ministry at Audenreid. When I left, she walked outside with me to say goodbye. Innocently, I reached over to kiss her goodbye, thinking it would be a long time until I would see her again. But she turned her face and said, "There it starts!" as if I were doing something immoral. I was hurt and offended.

I realized then that our friendship would never develop into a commitment, not understanding that the Lord had my true love and soul mate waiting for me. So, I wrote Jane my last letter. In it I confessed, "I had been hoping that our friendship would develop into a partnership for the Lord, but I now realize that you have your career and I have my calling. But I will always love you!" She answered, saying it was a sweet letter.

She did work in California for a year and then studied at Boston University School of Theology where her parents had studied. Jody joined her there and after graduation, they were ordained. Jane had planned to go to China as a missionary after graduation, but the door to China closed that year. Upon graduation, she moved to Florida as the associate pastor at the Wesley Foundation at Florida State University in Tallahassee, Fl. Later Jane was hired as dorm-mother for the Westminster Choir College in Princeton, N.J. After she married, she served as a Christian education director in Florida at more than one church. Jody spent several years raising her children and then ministered first as associate pastor and then as pastor of several churches and later as district superintendent. After retirement, she served churches as interim pastor and filled the pulpit from time to time.

Another step of faith came during my last two years at Drew when I was appointed pastor of two small churches near Hazelton, PA. I had never attended a church business meeting. Now I had to lead the business meeting in two churches. I was compelled to look to the Lord, again not leaning to my own understanding. Audenreid had about 50 in attendance and Jeanesville about 25. At one time, these had been thriving coal towns but as anthracite coal lost its market, the towns diminished to about one fourth of their former size. The people had a pessimistic outlook. The Jeanesville church felt about ready to close its doors.

However, wherever hungry hearts are receptive to the moving of the Holy Spirit, God blesses. His blessings came, not as the result of my ministry, but in spite of my weaknesses and failures. Without God's help, I could not have managed. Up to that time, I had preached in a church only five times. I had never attended an official board meeting but I was expected to officiate. I knew practically nothing about the machinery of the Methodist Church. However, God undertook, undergirded and worked through my blunders and mistakes. To see God work in spite of oneself is the greatest joy of serving Him. Since Seminary classes ended Friday at noon and began again on Tuesday, I was able to spend considerable time at the churches. Although I had an extremely busy schedule, I reveled in the work and was thrilled to see the Lord at work. Friday nights I held a prayer meeting in each of the churches. On Saturdays I prepared my sermon and held a joint youth meeting for both churches. Sunday mornings I preached in each church and did visitation in between. It was at Audenreid that I performed my first of several weddings.

A group from the Penn State Wesley Foundation led by Jody Montgomery made a presentation in my Audenreid church. It was refreshing to have another reminder from the Wesley Foundation, "A Home Away From Home," which had meant so much to me.

The pastor of the church in Woodbridge, Rev. William Justice, had been preparing copious notes, about his visit to Denmark. As he finished each segment, his secretary, Shirley, sent a copy to me. Then that first summer, Shirley and her aunt and uncle, with whom she lived, came to visit me at Audenreid. I felt a little taken back when Shirley brought me a pair of woolen socks that she had knitted. Later, her uncle said that she was interested in our relationship and wondered how I felt. How embarrassed I was when I had to reply that I considered her a friend but nothing more. Shirley was pretty, a good pianist and had secretarial training. She was a perfect candidate for a pastor's wife, but I was not in love with her. Again, the Lord was keeping me for the one and only partner He intended for me.

During my second summer at Audenreid, Child Evangelism summer missionaries asked if I could aid them in getting a place for their five-day clubs. I found several places at homes of our members. At the end of the time, the workers turned over a list of about twelve kids who had made decisions for Christ. I was able to follow up on them and invite their families to church. Later that summer, the Methodist Christian Education Director for the Conference had a meeting with some of us pastors. He warned us about Child Evangelism missionaries who were coming around. I told him in front of the others, "I don't care who wins the children for Christ, as long as they come to Him. Besides, they gave me a list of the ones who made decisions so I could follow up." That ended the warning!

At the conclusion of my time at Audenreid and Jeanesville, the people gave me a beautiful gold automatic wristwatch that I have to this day. Engraved on the back is "From Audenreid Church 1956."

AN UNEXPECTED NEW MINISTRY

While in my last year at Drew, I applied to the Methodist Mission Board. I had had numerous talks with the personnel secretary, Dr. M.O. Williams. As the result of his expressing the need for workers in Bolivia I decided to consider service among the Bolivian Indians. I prayed for the Lord's will in this matter, and did not seem to get any satisfaction of this being His calling, but I went ahead and applied nevertheless. Everything seemed to go smoothly, except for the uncertainty in my own heart. I went through all the tests and scored the highest IQ of any of the candidates, but my examiners objected to my answer to one question: "Who are you? How do you describe yourself?" My answer was "I am one whom the Lord changed. I was an introvert hoping to be in glass research. However, the Lord called me into His service and changed me. I now love to preach, teach, and minister to people. I see myself as one in whom the Lord Jesus lives and wants to express His life." Their evaluation: "You need to get down to earth." They must have thought I was too idealistic. They recommended that I take a two-year ministry before being considered further for the mission field. This was quite a blow because I was preparing to leave as soon as I got the OK. However, in retrospect, I can see God's hand behind this disappointing change: "In all things God works for the good of those who love Him, who have been called according to His purpose." The Lord was working this change in the road for my good and the ministry He had planned for me.

My District Superintendent assigned me to a four church charge near Bloomsburg, PA. He explained the situation and outlined what was expected of me during the two years I was to be at the charge. Earlier there had been seven churches with a senior pastor and an associate who had infrequent services at the churches. In an effort to strengthen the churches, the charge was divided. I got four churches: Jerseytown, Eyers Grove, Iola and Pine Summit. Some of the churches strongly resisted the change and threatened to stand in the way of the effectiveness of the charge. I was to help restore a friendly attitude among the churches and attempt to bring about more cooperation among them. The spiritual upbuilding of the charge and the purchase of a new parsonage were part of my responsibility. Being single allowed me to put my full time and attention in the ministry.

When I announced that each church would have a service every Sunday, one lady declared that she could not believe that they could have that much church! I was on a circuit, and every Sunday had a service in each of three churches and then preached a different sermon in the fourth church in the evening, to which all the churches were invited. The combined attendance at the four churches was about two hundred. To be fair to all the churches, I made out a monthly schedule and rotated for each church to have the prized 11 AM service. Sunday Schools then adapted to the schedule. I held two prayer meetings on Wednesday night and two on Thursday night. At the confirmation classes, many young people accepted Christ as their personal Savior.

In order to coordinate all the activities of the four churches, I enlisted volunteers from each church to help put together a monthly newspaper. We had a reporter, a secretary who did the stencil, an assembler and a distributor in each church. After the news was gathered and stencils cut, I mimeographed the pages, which were assembled and distributed in each church. After a contest, we chose the name "The Trumpet."

We held three Vacation Bible Schools in the summer with total attendance approaching two hundred.

From the beginning of October through the end of November, we held nightly revival services, two weeks in each church. The members of all four churches were invited to the church holding the services that week. How many came to Christ during those meetings, only eternity will tell. Many responded to the invitation to come forward to accept Christ. Joe and Georgeanne Lane, have kept in touch through the years. Georgeanne always dates her conversion to one of those meetings. I had guest speakers for some of the weeks, including my seminary roommate Bob Carruthers. (I later also spent a week preaching in his church for a week of revival services.) A young Methodist evangelist also took part in one of my churches another week. Both men went with me to visit people and encourage them to come out to the meetings. It was a glorious time! As a result of the campaign, the spiritual life of the church seemed to deepen.

If I got one night a month free during my time at the Jerseytown-Eyers Grove Charge, I considered myself fortunate.

The first summer, I rented a room from a lovely old lady, Mrs. Gardner, mother of one of the church members. Mrs. Gardner was shocked when I announced that I was going to take a vacation. She thought that a pastor should not take a vacation away from the church. She commented, "God doesn't take a vacation." I replied, "No, but I am not God." For my vacation, I went to Word of Life Camp in the Adirondack Mountains and stayed on the Island where there was an excellent program for young people. I wanted to see what it was like so that the following summer, I might take a group of youth there. Little did I realize that the love of my life was the Bible teacher at the "Ranch," a junior camp a few miles away!

TOWARD MY GOAL

more schooling

During the time at these churches, I still had my eye on my calling to be a missionary. Because of the way the Methodist Missionary Officials had questioned that which was so important in my life, that is, my personal relationship with Jesus, I decided that I did not want to serve under the Methodist Mission Board. So, I enrolled in Moody Bible Institute in the Missionary Course as a special student.

The time at the churches was invaluable, but I felt the need to move on. Because I liked the work and the people so much, it would not have been difficult from a human standpoint to stay and minister another 10 years. But, I began to feel the desire to attend a Bible Institute to further my training in two important areas. First, I felt I needed to know the Bible better. I felt woefully lacking in many respects where the Word of God was concerned. Secondly, I wanted to take courses in missionary strategy and medicine, which I felt were essential. I really hated to give up the work on the charge. At times, even after I informed the charge of my plans, I vacillated and was strongly tempted to change my plans. Only the conviction that the Lord was leading me to Moody prevented me.

Two problems made the change more difficult. I wanted to leave knowing that I had fulfilled my obligations. The charge had no parsonage for a family. Secondly, there was no pastor available just then to take my place. However, the Lord did not leave these two areas undone. I had agreed to stay through the summer before I left for Moody. Just a month before school was to begin, I found a new and beautiful parsonage, which all four churches were able to agree on. Added to this blessing and even more important, two weeks before school was to begin, a minister who was leaving the chaplaincy agreed to take the charge. It was a lesson in faith to me and to the people of the churches. The Lord worked it out at the last minute! I left the charge feeling that my work was done: the churches were cooperating, people were growing in the Lord, a beautiful parsonage was ready for a new minister and his family and best of all, the Lord was working through and among the people. What a wonderful assurance of God's leading me to Moody!

The people of the churches gathered to say farewell. Eyes welled up with tears as we shook hands. Their appreciation, well wishes, prayers and gifts meant so much to me. As I departed, I was not aware that my childhood friend, George Pepper, had moved to Bloomsburg where he set up a dental practice about the same time I left the area.

AN ORDINATION

that almost did not happen

In the Methodist Church, there are three possible ordinations. The first is as Deacon, the second as Elder and, for a favorite few, the third is as Bishop. A year before I had been ordained as Deacon, and now in 1957, I was scheduled to be ordained as Elder. I appeared before the Examining Board who reviewed my record and considered my plans. They asked if I agreed with the Methodist doctrine. I answered that at one point, I have difficulties. I believe that the Bible teaches baptism by immersion for believers, but says nothing about sprinkling or pouring for babies. I also told them that I was going to go to Moody Bible Institute and would probably be a missionary under another organization. They asked how I would feel if they held up my ordination until such a time that I should come back into the Methodist ministry. I agreed that such a decision was fair. So, the recommendation came before the entire Methodist Conference consisting of pastors and delegates from all the churches in the Central Pennsylvania Conference.

But the District Superintendent, who at that time was Dr. Montgomery, Jane's father, who had been my pastor at the Wesley Foundation, suggested that I leave the room while the conference delegates could discuss the situation. Then he argued that my record as pastor was excellent and, as my District Superintendent, he felt that my previous record should be the criteria for ordination. The conference took a vote and I was declared eligible for ordination.

Later that day, we stood in line to be questioned by Bishop Oxnam about our obedience to the rules for pastors: "Do you refrain from strong drink and do you refrain from smoking tobacco?" Each candidate said, "yes" except the one standing by me. He replied, "I do smoke." "Well," said the bishop, "Say 'yes' with mental reservations."

An interesting side note is that I stayed in a home in Curwensville, Pa, a few miles from Clearfield where the conference was held. My future wife lived in Curwensville, less than a mile away! For the second time, I was close to the one with whom I would later spend the rest of my life.

Chapter 4

From Seminary to Bible Institute

It must have seemed strange for Moody Bible Institute to enroll a seminary graduate in a Bible School. The famous evangelist, Dwight L. Moody, founded the school. He wanted it to be located in a slum area of Chicago in order to reach those in most need. Since I enrolled as a special student, I was able to take just the courses I wanted. I chose mostly Bible, evangelism and missionary courses and took the maximum of twenty hours. To improve my singing ability, I joined the men's glee club. In the afternoons, I worked at the Greater Europe Mission headquarters. In addition, Saturday mornings I worked for a Jewish couple cleaning their home and their windows twenty stories above the street. At that time, I had no idea how Greater Europe Mission would enter into my future plans, but the Lord was leading all the way.

At the beginning of the second semester, my advisor, Dr. Harold Cook, suggested that I could graduate in a year if I took six additional Christian work assignments to meet the requirements for graduation. Moody could give me credit for some of my seminary work. The first semester I had two Christian work assignments, but now I was going to have six, in addition to nineteen hours of class work. But, what a blessing those assignments were! I did Spanish visitation, Cook County Hospital visitation, rescue mission work, counseling at an orphanage, boy's Sunday School class and street evangelism. It was an important year of learning and experience that would serve me well as a missionary. Some of what was lacking in my seminary experience was made up here.

I had one experience of Moody's strict rules. I took a girl to a concert and then to dinner. As the curfew time drew near, I asked the waiter for the dinner bill. It was a long time in coming, so we had to rush back to Moody. We were two minutes late! The next day, I was called in by my counselor and reprimanded. What an embarrassment for a pastor who had been in the ministry for more than four years! I guess the Lord knew I needed more humbling.

Every year a "Sadie Hawkins" day was held, where the girls could invite the boys to a dinner. A sister of Gareth Sweatman invited me. Gareth was a spiritual boy and I had prayed with him in his room on several occasions. I had seen his good-looking sister, Dorie, but I thought she seemed like a flirt. He had suggested that she invite me to the Sadie Hawkins dinner. I was impressed with her zeal for the Lord and a challenge she put before me: when I told her about the young people in my church that had come to Christ, she asked, "What are you doing to follow up?" I was not doing anything and her question got me thinking.

During the summer following graduation, I enrolled in two special classes: one on Bible Institute work and the other on writing Christian literature. At the time, I met Paul Peasley who was intending to start a Bible Institute in Puebla, Mexico for the Central American Mission. That interested me since I liked teaching and became acquainted with that kind of work done by the Greater Europe Mission. Doris and Larry were missionaries in Mexico under the Mexican Indian Mission. My discussions with them, along with several visits to Mexico helped burden my heart for the country. I applied to Central America Mission (CAM) and was invited to candidate school in Dallas, Texas.

One day we were exposed to what life in the jungle could be like. They took us to an isolated spot, gave us a chicken and told us that we had to kill, pluck, cook and eat it. We were also given horseback riding lessons. I had never ridden a horse by myself, so I asked if I could take the horse for a ride after the instruction period. I galloped him down a country road toward an old farmhouse, then turned him around and headed back to the camp. But, he refused to go and kept turning around and heading back to the farm. Finally, in frustration, I got off and led him to the camp. Then I found out that the farm was his home and he thought he was finished with us amateurs!

CAM accepted me and I began deputation. With an interdenominational mission, candidates have to make their own contacts and travel to various churches to present their vision. Now I faced the problem of raising support. I did not have many contacts, and I needed to earn $700 to pay off school debts. I called the Methodist Superintendent, who then was Dr. Montgomery, and asked if possibly I could serve a small church while raising funds. He agreed to take me to Gordon, a small town just two miles from Ashland where I grew up. It was a church that I had been in before when my friend David Davies, who at that time lived in Gordon, would go to the church to practice on the piano and I tagged along. I had also been in a minstrel with him on behalf of the Gordon fire company. I met with the friendly leaders and seriously considered accepting the position.

When we returned to the Montgomery home in Sunbury, they invited me to stay overnight because Jane was coming home the next day. They were quite insistent, countering my excuse that I did not have pajamas or my shaver, with offers to use Dr. Montgomery's. But not wanting to get my heart involved again, I declined and drove home to Williamsport. The Lord was again leading me to the love of my life, my lifetime partner.

I had also applied to Moody Press for a job at the Institute. When I got word that they accepted my application, I called Dr. Montgomery to thank him and to say that I was going to work at Moody Press. I thought that I could not only earn money to pay off my debt, but I could learn more about evangelical Christian literature that would help me in the future. Perhaps I could also raise some support while there.

Bruce Johnson—a former Moody student whom I had helped with lessons—and I rented an apartment on LaSalle Street. Later he asked if a man he had met could live in with us and pay part of the rent. The man, Jim, was an ex-convict who had professed Christ but who was living in fear of the Mafia.

We lived together for about a year and then broke apart. I rented a small bedroom and lived by myself for the remainder of the time in Chicago.

Ken Taylor was the head of Moody Press. Knowing my interest in literature, he invited me to sit in on an editorial board meeting where decisions were made about what books to print. He also invited the whole Moody Press staff to his home for a hayride. While at his home, he asked me if I had had a teacher at Drew by the name of Howard Kee. He was one of the most brilliant graduates of Dallas Seminary and was prompted by Wilbur Smith to go on for a doctorate in a liberal seminary, then to come out unscathed as an evangelical testimony to the scholarly world. However, he did not come out unscathed and embraced Neo Orthodox theology. At Drew, he was the professor who, because of my evangelical viewpoint, said, "You should loosen up."

My job at Moody Press felt like a great letdown from being a pastor: I filled orders to be sent out to bookstores and colporteurs. I walked and walked among those aisles of books and was exhausted at the end of the day. But I found time to study Greek by correspondence with Judson College. It was difficult to do it without a teacher present and especially to master the pronunciation.

I had several opportunities to preach and teach while working at Moody Press. For four Sundays, I preached at the YMCA and for several months taught a Bible Study at a Servicemen's Center at the Great Lakes Naval Training Center.

A MISTAKE ALMOST MADE

At Christmas break, before I drove home to Pennsylvania, I posted a notice on the board to invite students to ride along with me. Dorie Sweatman was one of my passengers. I dropped her off in Harrisburg and the others at their homes before driving to Williamsport. After the Christmas vacation, only Dorie Sweatman planned to return with me to Moody. We ran into a fierce snowstorm and crept along mile after mile. At one stop, she leaned over for me to kiss her. I did. After that, I began to date her and gave her my Penn State ring to wear.

The following summer I organized a Spanish visitation team and enlisted Mrs. Solis to teach us Spanish. She was a small, sweet Mexican lady who went to apartments, climbed the stairs, dressed the children and like the Pied Piper, led them to Sunday School.

Dorie went with "Send the Light" mission to Mexico. They planned to take two truckloads of Christian literature. Missionaries had cautioned the young people of this group of the difficulties in getting Christian literature across the border. It seemed like a miracle that they were able to get across undetected. They also established a bookstore in Mexico City and advertised it over the radio. Christian broadcasts were forbidden, but advertising was permitted.

However, Dorie became ill with colitis in Mexico. In fact, she had to leave Moody because of her illness, so I offered to drive her home to Harrisburg. I felt sorry for her because I thought perhaps she went there because I was headed to Mexico and she wanted to see what it was like. Even though our friendship was not without frequent disagreements, I liked Dorie and respected her desire to serve the Lord. At Christmas I proposed marriage and she accepted. I completed my work at Moody and her family was able to intercede to get me a good paying job as a laboratory assistant at AMP Inc. in Harrisburg, PA. My immediate boss went to the same church as the Sweatmans. And the Sweatmans invited me to live in one of their rooms and pay for room and board.

This was a stormy time for us. Dorie was nine years younger than I, and I think the age difference was a problem. We frequently argued and it is now apparent that the Lord used the situation to prevent us from making a big mistake. I had a habit of pushing my glasses up when they slipped down and clearing my throat. That annoyed her, but a deviated septum gave me throat problems, and I couldn't seem to help it. She also considered me too laid back. She was much more aggressive in personality, and I thought she was too bold and critical. The situation became intolerable. I felt obligated to marry her, since I had promised and was engaged. But I felt locked in. I prayed and asked for an answer and the Lord gave me the verse in Exodus 14:13 "stand still and see the salvation of the Lord!"

One day Dorie, with an annoyed look on her face, was mocking me again by mimicking some of my habits: clearing my throat and pushing my glasses up my nose. Her mother saw it and said, "Dorie, stop that!" and an argument ensued between them. She was well aware of the problems we were having. Mrs. Sweatman struggled with Dorie and threw her down on the floor. Dorie rose to attack me with fists flying.

Mrs. Sweatman shouted for her to stop, but I said "Don't worry, she can't hurt me." Then she put a deep scratch in my neck and, crying, headed up the stairs. Her mother shouted, "Give him back the ring." Dorie threw it down the stairs. To me this broke the engagement and my obligation to fulfill my promise to marry her. Because of all the trouble, I had earlier decided to move out and had rented a room in Harrisburg. So when Mrs. Sweatman said, "You had better get another place to live," I was able to say, "I already have a place." I realized that living in the same house with her had been part of the problem, although it was good to have seen the potential of a stormy marriage.

Dorie asked for her diamond ring back, but I would not give it to her. I think she hated to give up the ring, even though we both were in agreement to break the engagement. Earlier I had felt that I had to live up to my promise to marry her, but now I was free! We did meet several times after that to talk, but it was obvious that the Lord did not mean us for each other.

Shortly after our breakup, I went to an ear nose and throat specialist about my throat problem. He suggested it was my deviated septum and an operation would help. I had the deviation since I was two years old when I had fallen down concrete steps and broken my nose. After the operation, as I was recuperating in the hospital, I met Tommy, whom the nurses were encouraging to walk after his appendicitis operation. I helped the reluctant 12 year-old and walked with him down the halls. When I explained the gospel to him, he told me about the Jehovah's witnesses who were teaching his mother and grandmother. I warned him about their false teaching and he said he wished I would speak with his mother, Elona. I had hoped to meet her when he was released, but I missed her and she and Tommy left before I could meet her. He had given me his telephone number; as soon as I was released, I called Elona. She reluctantly agreed for me to come. I studied up on the teaching of the Witnesses and was prepared, trusting in the Lord's help, as I arrived at her home.

Tommy, his mother and his grandmother were waiting for me. She seemed ready for a fight. I explained that Jesus was God in the flesh and that he died on the cross to save us from our sins—but we had to make a conscious decision to accept Him. The Lord gave me verses that I shared with her. The Holy Spirit touched Elona's heart and she began to weep. She said she had invited me to set me straight, but now the Lord was dealing with her. She asked if I could come back when the Jehovah's Witnesses came to teach her. I happily agreed.

When the time came the following week, I insisted that we pray in Jesus' name. As we dealt with Bible verses, I made the couple keep in the context. I kept emphasizing that Jesus was God in the flesh, who came to die for our sins. At the end of the meeting, in frustration, they asked if I could come next week when the district superintendent would come.

The following week, he came with another couple along as well. Again I insisted we pray in Jesus' name and emphasized the Bible verses that showed His divinity. Again the Lord was present and the Holy Spirit spoke to Elona's heart. After they left, she said, "I do not need to see them again. I know now that they are false teachers." However, we had agreed to meet once more. This time I invited the pastor of the church I attended, Pastor Howard Burtner, to meet with us. Only the two couples without their superintendent came that week. Pastor Burtner was used of the Lord to affect one of the couples, who said when we parted, "We would like to visit your church." Elona, her husband Jim, her grandmother and Tommy began attending a Bible teaching church. I also held several Bible study sessions in their home and they became part of our support team while we were in Sweden.

When I decided that I needed to get on with raising my support to go to Mexico, I turned in my resignation. The boss asked me to stay on as an engineer at a fine salary, but God had other plans.

I decided to take a week of vacation at Word of Life Inn in the Adirondacks after finishing my work at AMP. I thought that I also might make some good contacts for support. When I called to make reservations, I was disappointed to find there were no vacancies that I could afford. I asked the receptionist to call me if there was a cancellation in the cheaper rooms.

Weeks went by, and I had decided that Word of Life was out of the question. Then, two days before the camp was to begin, I received a call that there was a vacancy. To decide to go or not to go seemed like a very small decision to make in light of the expectation of going to Mexico to help start a Bible Institute. I hesitated for what seemed to be a long time and wondered if I was imposing on the caller. "Oh well," I said, "I was not planning to go at this late date, but yes, I will be there." That small decision changed my life forever!

Living in the center of God's will is vital to making the right decisions. How easy it would be to miss the best that God has for us. Proverbs 3:5-6 has often been applied to my life: "Trust in the Lord with all your heart and lean not on your own understanding; in all your ways acknowledge him and he will make your paths straight" or "he will direct your paths."

Our home in Ashland; Doris, Dad, Mother and me; Doris and me as Scouts; play time with Doris; Doris and I were very close; Jackie, Craig, Doris and Jeannie at Berry's Grove.

Boat built by Bill- the Verna May; boyhood friend David Davies; friends George and Jeannie Pepper at Berry's Grove; ROTC dance with Mary Ellen Boyer; all together- me with sisters Ruth, Doris, Harvena and Betty..

Jane, Dr. Montgomery and Jody; Queen Jane, tuxedoless Bill and friends; Drew friends: Himes, Jackson, Carruthers, Johnson; Woodbridge youth group; VBS in Jerseytown; Audenreid wedding; Doris and Larry on the way to the mission field.

II

Chapter 5

"Born to Tell"

"Roses on my shoulders, blue slippers on my feet. I'm Mama's little darling. Don't you think I'm sweet?" So began Evelyn Roberts desire to entertain when she was three years old. Her older sisters would take her to their one room school, put her on a desk and have her sing to the class.

Ruth Evelyn Roberts was born to use her gift in acting to help others. She was completely in touch with her own identity. "Born to Tell" was the title she chose for her story. Having the main part in all the school plays gave her the opportunity to develop her skills at entertaining. Even into old age, she could recall some of the parts like "I'm Sunbonnet Sue and I'm busy from morning to night." "Oh, Doctor come, my doll's sick with the flu. It must be the flu because her arms flew and her legs flew and her head flew. What else could it be but the flu?" She enjoyed pointing her finger at me as she recited, "Smarty, smarty, smarty. Thought you'd have a party. Remember what the teacher taught. You'll be sorry if you get caught . . . ." Sometimes after a play, people would put her on their shoulders and pass her from one to another. She was talented, beautiful, popular—shining almost too brightly for her small town.

She remembers sitting in the grassy field, looking up at the sky dreaming about becoming an actress until an experience at thirteen set the course of her life.

She was born on March 20,1927, on a farm in Braselton Georgia, a town with a population of 165. The family lived in a small and cold farmhouse and eked out a living during the depression. Although they were very poor, they always had plenty to eat. Evelyn helped in any way she could: milking cows, feeding chickens and pigs and hoeing cotton. After a hot and tiring day of picking cotton, her father would help pull her home with his hoe.

Evelyn's father, Earley Roberts, was a handsome friendly man, who often took time from his farm work to talk to people. His generosity sometimes deprived his family of needed money. However, his love for people was passed on down to Evelyn.

Earley fell in love with and courted beautiful Esther Duck, but she was only fifteen. Her father, William Duck, Pastor of the Zion Baptist Church, discouraged the relationship, but the young couple could not wait until she got older, so, to her parents chagrin, they eloped.

Esther worked hard to provide a nice home for her family, but the small house Earley purchased was in ill repair. She made the best of it, even though wind blew into cracks in the house and the roof leaked. Evelyn remembered hearing her mother say, "Earley, you have got to stop that roof from leaking!"

Esther had eight children—five girls and three boys, all born at home—Evelyn was the fifth. As the family grew, the girls had to share beds, cuddling up to one another. Every morning Esther made biscuits for Earley to take to work, but she was frequently sick. When Evelyn got older, she took over and made the biscuits and all the children did the housework.

Her mother had told her, "You were a hard baby to wean from the breast." Evelyn remarking about her mother's love said, "A little cup with kittens on it sits on our living room mantle." Her mother had used that charming cup to wean Evelyn and the cup had become one of her most precious possessions. Evelyn continued, "The cup tells the story that my mother was loving, patient, wise and full of ideas which might accomplish the thing desired without too much stress."

In order to help, the older children took care of the younger. Mildred, five years older than Evelyn, cared for her. When Evelyn was bad, Mildred would scare her. Evelyn recalls, "That had the desired effect, but it caused me to be easily frightened later. Mildred was jealous of my curly hair so she cut it."

In her autobiography Evelyn continued, "In spite of these seemingly minor disorders, we were a big happy family. Together, we ate our good southern food of corn bread, milk and boiled vegetables. We slept together, three in a bed when it was necessary. We played together in playhouses, the woods and in the big barn. A certain climb up the ladder to the loft in the barn in search of the newborn kittens was thrilling until I stepped on a pitch fork!" It was very cold in the winter when she went to the outhouse. Sears catalog served as toilet paper.

Along with the farm work, Evelyn helped with her younger brothers, Earl and Billy, and her sister, Damaris. She loved to tell stories to her brothers and sister, stories about children. She was also very concerned about them. Earley, Jr. had a hard time with his studies in elementary school. Evelyn spent many hours tutoring him and massaging his severe leg cramps. It was hard for him to walk down the road to catch the school bus. Sometimes Evelyn would carry him. Though he was six years younger than Evelyn was, Earl and she were very close. Damaris had "soft spot" in her head that sometimes caused her to fall and she did not know where she was. Evelyn was concerned that Billy picked up cigarette butts to smoke. She told her dad to make him stop. He was concerned as well, but he couldn't do much about it.

Not all was work on that dusty little farm. As a toddler, she made mud pies under the watering trough, even after Aunt Mae scolded her for getting so dirty. Evelyn tells about sitting in the peach tree and enjoying ripe fruit while the juice ran down her chin. Eating figs from their fig tree was a special delight.

From time to time, Evelyn's father hired men of color to help with the farming. Evelyn used to like to help some of the older black people with their chores. Evelyn told about her experiences with the hired hands: "Lije, helped us in the home and with the children. He helped get the children ready for school, and Earl liked him so much that he would not let anyone else help him with his shoes."

Evelyn continued, "One day, a man came walking along the road. He said he hadn't anything to eat except wild plums.

Father hired him to help with the farm work and told him that he could sleep in a little hut across the road. At night you could hear him loudly praying before he went to bed. Every day I sneaked up there to clean his room and make his bed after he had gone to work. I was surprised to find a gun under his bed. Mother would not have liked my going there at all but she didn't know about it. One day Hector went away. We didn't know where he had gone and we never saw him again."

She and her sisters liked to fish. One day they got a seine and an old telephone and scared the fish into their net. Then they built a fire and ate their fresh catch. But a game warden caught them at this illegal way of fishing and fined them.

Mrs. Roberts "dipped snuff." Evelyn remembers, "I was curious about how it tasted and said 'Let me try it.' I put some under my tongue. Then I got very sick and lay on the porch and spit and spit. I didn't do that any more! That was the end of snuff for me! I also got deathly sick from the medicine I was given for worms. They thought I was going to die, but the Lord had other plans."

At Christmas, she got oranges, a box of candy sticks and a tiny little celluloid baby. When it got cold and icicles formed, she put them in a glass with milk for a frosty. She chewed twigs from a sweet gum tree to make a toothbrush.

Evelyn liked to reminisce: "As I look back to school days, I wish I had greater incentives to make me study. I don't believe I did much of this because I could keep up with the rest of my class without much studying. I was never pleased unless I made at least a ninety on my graded papers. I was one of the three highest in my class as far as grades went. Intermingled with school, there were friends, parties, and times of relaxing. I would sit in a peach tree eating delicious, juicy peaches. There were times of bumping to church in a wagon. Sometimes we would hang our feet over the edge of the wagon from the back or jump off and run alongside."

A story went around that the old Duncan house, just down the road from the Robert's farm, was haunted. It was reported that the long dead Duncans were seen there. Evelyn's brother Julien liked to scare her with tales told about the haunted house and about a treasure supposedly buried there.

One dark night, after she stayed too long at a friend's house, a heavy mist cast strange shadows over the field she had to cross. She always hurried across the field, sometimes thinking about the nearby Duncan house. This night, in the distance she saw an apparition which seemed to appear from nowhere. It was all white and fluttered in the wind. The figure drew nearer saying "Hoo, hoo." She ran home, terrified, as fast as her legs would carry her. After she got home and caught her breath, the front door opened slowly and her older sisters stood there, holding a white sheet in their arms.

She also spent a frightful night, feeling that the devil was standing there by her bedside. Witches were a topic of conversation and it was said that people called upon witches to get the cows to milk.

Chapter 6

A Vision of Her Mission in Life

When Evelyn was thirteen, something happened that radically changed the course of her life. She had been troubled with feelings of guilt, afraid she might die and go to Hell. She went with her Bible to a gully to pray, but she did not understand what to do or what should happen. She thought everyone was supposed to be saved like Paul. In her own words, she said, "I went on a search to find out what life was all about and how to go to Heaven. I didn't have far to go in the search. I went in a wagon with my mother and the children to a Methodist church, New Liberty, far out in the country. There I went forward and told a man in charge that I needed to be saved. But they didn't tell me how. There was a man, Uncle Warren, who said 'I think you'd better be baptized.' Nevertheless, that didn't seem to help anything. My oldest sister, Velma, said, 'We are going to have revival next week in our Baptist Church.' So, I went home with her and then to the church. The people who wanted to be saved went up front and sat on a mourner's bench. They were supposed to 'pray through'. But I never understood how to do that. Velma's husband, Webster, said 'Come and I will show you how to get saved.' He took me on his lap and showed me Acts 16:31 'Believe on the Lord Jesus Christ and thou shalt be saved and thy house.' Webster asked, 'Don't you believe Jesus died for your sins and rose again?' Yes! I replied!" And when the truth of the Word of God had sunk in, she said, in her picturesque way, "My sins just went rolling away and I knew that I was forgiven and had become a child of God."

Afterward, as she was praying, she told the Lord, "Now I don't want to be an actress; I want to be a missionary to tell others how they can get to Heaven!" Everyone who knew her felt that Evelyn, with her stunning beauty and ability to charm her audience, would have become a famous actress. The name "Evelyn" means "light," and she certainly lived up to her name: There was a happy sparkle about her. However, the Lord wanted to use her gifts, personality and dedication to win children and others to Him.

Evelyn and her cousins, Howard, Lurline and Ruby Dean Duck, sang together in area churches and at hymn sings. She had a lovely voice with perfect pitch and the ability to sing harmony without notes or accompaniment.

In High School, Evelyn had a boyfriend named James Coffee. Although he was her good friend, their relationship was not very serious. He asked her to marry him, but her answer was, "No, I am going to be a missionary."

OFF TO SCHOOL

"... in all your ways acknowledge him and He will direct your path"

Evelyn was anxious to get her training for missionary service, and some local women offered to send her to Martha Berry, a Methodist college. However, her sister, Lola, had moved to Toccoa Falls and told her about a Bible School in the town. Toccoa Falls Bible College was an excellent school to train her for the mission field.

She had no money but a lot of faith. Superintendent Kelley Barnes, an imposing figure with his crop of red hair, met her for an interview. "I would like to study here, but I have no money. Could I work at the school to pay my way?" "We don't normally give work scholarships to first year students, but we will make an exception for you." He was no doubt impressed by her faith and commitment to be a missionary.

Evelyn worked at least 35 hours a week for that scholarship. Many times she fell asleep on her books. She peeled potatoes, cooked food, worked at the switchboard, at the snack shack and finally was put in charge of supervising the cleaning crew.

At one point she worked in President Dr. R. A. Forest's home and cooked for him and his wife. Dr. Forrest was a gracious man and only laughed when she cooked liver in a pressure cooker and served shoe leather tough meat! Finally, in her last year, a dentist paid her way.

Mr. Barnes had a nephew who was in the Navy but who did not know the Lord. He asked Evelyn to make friends with Benfer in order to lead him to Christ. He was a handsome, artistic fellow, with brown, wavy hair. She met him in her usual friendly way and they became great friends. After a while, other students considered them a couple on campus. She used to sing, "I love my sailor boy and he loves me too." Evelyn continued to try to help him receive the Lord, but apparently, he did not respond. Her zeal for the Lord was too much for him and she needed someone who loved and served the Lord, so their relationship did not continue.

Sometimes, when she got hungry, she went to her sister Lola's home for a snack. But if she and Robert were not home, Evelyn would find an unlocked window and climb in. Lola fondly says, "We could always tell when Evelyn had been there because she left the peanut butter jar open on the table!"

Summer vacation came, and needing money badly for school, she wondered about where she could get a job. Her roommate told her about an aunt who was just starting a business in Birmingham, Alabama and needed help.

They boarded a bus expecting to be involved in this new business startup. It was exciting to travel to this big city and experience a welcome change from studying. However, when they got off the bus, they discovered that the aunt's business never got started. Now they did not have a job or a place to stay. A bus driver helped them find a room to rent and they found a job at Britlin's Cafeteria. The bus driver dated this beautiful, friendly new arrival. But that was short-lived when she found out he was married!

Her beauty and personality won her many friends and favor at Toccoa, and before she graduated, she was chosen, along with Charles Good, a fellow student, to represent the school in their publicity literature.

Chapter 7

Out Into Ministry

While in college, Evelyn attended the Oriental Missionary group meetings and had a burden for Japan. When she graduated, she applied to the Far Eastern Gospel Crusade for service there. She was disappointed when the director wrote that because she was single and very young, he could not send her out with the mission.

Seeking the ministry the Lord had for her, she accepted a position at a rescue mission in Savannah, Georgia. As she sat on the bus on the way, she thought about the many things she could do in life, but said "If didn't give myself to the Lord, nothing would come of it. So I gave my hands, my feet, my eyes, my lips, my head and my heart—every part of my body—to the Lord."

She lived with the Aiken family, who operated the mission, and received a salary of $50 a month and room and board. "The children were the most important to me," she said with the usual enthusiasm that bubbled up whenever she thought about children. Evelyn taught at the mission youth camp from

June through August 1948. She led many children to the Lord. Her own brother, Billy, accepted the Lord under her ministry at camp. She conducted Bible clubs and helped in the mission meetings.

Both at the mission and at the summer camps, her joy was leading children to Christ and teaching them Bible verses and singing songs like "Lift up your heads oh ye gates . . ." She said, "I thought that was a grand thing to do." In addition, she led in singing at the rescue mission's services and even spoke to the men about Jesus and His ability to save them and deliver them from addiction to alcohol. One man had been a wealthy businessman with a wife and two nice children. His drinking caused his family to leave him. He was found drunk in a ditch before he came to the mission.

She recalled one vivid image of Savannah, "I did not easily forget the Bonaventure Cemetery. To me it was like a cave with stalactites and stalagmites and a reminder of the shortness of life."

At one point she had an accident with the mission car but she was afraid to tell the director, George Aiken, so she arranged to have it repaired without telling him. Apparently, he was a controlling person and she feared what he would say.

On one occasion, she went downtown to a hat shop. She says, "I loved hats and would spend my last penny for a hat. I tried on a nice hat and the woman saw that I liked it. She gave it to me! I made very little money; I liked that hat and I was glad to have it." Mr. Aiken reprimanded her for accepting the hat as a gift. He said, "We could have bought a hat for you."

Perhaps he felt it was a reflection on the low wages Evelyn was getting.

A STEP OF FAITH ALONG THE WAY

After a fruitful 2-1/2 years, Evelyn was invited to go to Pennsylvania to a Child Evangelism training school in Pittsburgh. To meet this challenging opportunity, this little Georgia servant of the Lord took another huge step of faith, traveled to Pittsburgh and enrolled in the school. On the bus going there, she felt very, very cold and had only a short coat. She always wanted a long coat with a fur collar. One of her new friends had several coats and gave one to Evelyn. It was just the style she wanted and she loved it! The Lord provided for the cold in a special and loving way.

Evelyn enthusiastically took in the teaching about reaching children through Child Evangelism, and to her teacher, Miss Piet who trained young women to go out to different counties as Child Evangelism Directors.

While at the school, Evelyn attended a local Presbyterian Church. The pastor, several years older than she, took an interest in this beautiful Georgia belle. He asked her out on a date and they toured Penn State University. Once, after Evelyn had returned to her home for a visit, the pastor drove all the way to Braselton, Georgia to meet her family. He later proposed marriage to her, but she was not interested.

Miss Piet, a stern but kindly woman was impressed by Evelyn's zeal and ability and had great hopes for her. She sent her to Cambria County, PA to develop a Child Evangelism ministry there. There she met Roxie Grove, began training her and they both traveled all over the county meeting with pastors and setting up "Five Day Clubs." Hundreds of children made decisions for Christ during that time. The ministry she developed continues to this day. Besides recruiting and training workers, Evelyn held Good News clubs. A typical report from September 1950 when she started to March 1951 showed 421 children reached with 110 decisions for Christ. The year she left, there were 427 decisions.

During the time she worked in Cambria County, she went by bus to California to a Child Evangelism conference, where she met with other workers and got further training. After the long bus trip, she was constipated, and the host in the home where she stayed recommended a Christian Chiropractor who, she said, could help her. However, Evelyn felt that the visit to the chiropractor, who used an electric instrument on her internally, was responsible for her life-long fight with ulcerative colitis.

July 1953, after Evelyn's work in Cambria was completed, Miss Piet sent her to Clearfield County, PA to develop a new work. She met with the board and began settling in. She was given a car to drive, but the meager wages of $100/month she received as CEF Director made it difficult for her to find a place to live. A board member, Ansel Beers, invited her to live with him and his wife on their farm in Rochton. They were away at their music store every day and she didn't like living in a big house by herself. His wife was not pleased with the arrangements, and Evelyn sensed the resentment, so she decided she could not live there.

She packed her bag and left not knowing where she would end up. Evelyn was a people person and dreaded the thought of living alone. When she visited people in her ministry, she hoped that someone would invite her to spend the night. One day she visited another board member, Arthur Schirmer and his wife Audrey in Curwensville. When they understood her circumstance, they invited her to stay overnight in their hallway, which had a bed and a desk. This went on for several days. Each day she would pack her suitcase and go out to work. Then they invited her to move in with them. She said, "That was a great day because I wasn't so lonely anymore."

She stayed with them for seven years. The Schirmer's daughter, who had been a nurse on her way to Bible school to train to be missionary, was drowned in the ocean at Harvey Cedars Christian camp. That happened just one year before Evelyn showed up. They found her to be a great help in their grief and began to consider her a daughter. Her time with them was a welcome and satisfying refuge and she melted into this new family. They treated her like a real daughter and at bedtime, Mr. Schirmer would ask, "Where's my goodnight kiss?" She would peck him on the cheek as his daughter had done. Evelyn enjoyed traveling with the Schirmers to Pittsburgh to Kaufman's department store and shopping for clothes with Mrs. Schirmer. She loved to have all her clothes coordinated and topped off with a lovely hat.

Mr. Schirmer had a ministry in the county jail and Evelyn enjoyed going with him to witness to the inmates. One inmate sewed a "Grab Bag" for her to use in her ministry. Through the years, Evelyn used the Grab Bag to teach verses to the children. When the child learned a verse, she was able to reach down in the bag and get a prize.

Evelyn got the Child Evangelism ministry started and it grew and grew. Many children came to the Lord. Donna Smouse was one of the women she trained and who traveled with her all over the county up and down the hills for four years to visit churches, hold children's meetings and teacher classes.

Chapter 8

Word Of Life

Mr. Schirmer had recently received the Lord under Jack Wyrtzen and his ministry in New York City, so he was interested in Jack's Word of Life camp ministry. He arranged for Evelyn to accompany him to Word of Life with the intent of her being a summer counselor. She hesitated because she wanted to stay in Clearfield County as Child Evangelism Director. There were many clubs, teachers had been trained, and the Lord was doing a great work there through young people who wanted to be teachers. However, she went with him to the Ranch, a Word of Life Junior camp. When they arrived, to her embarrassment, Mr. Schirmer put all her teaching materials on the ground at the Junior Camp headquarters. Jack Wyrtzen, the founder and director of the work, saw the materials and invited her to be the Ranch Bible teacher. It was an opportunity to reach hundreds of young people every week all summer long.

As the "cowgirl," she wore a cowgirl hat, white cowgirl boots and gorgeous suits. One suit was purple and intricately embroidered and the other was gold and covered in fringe and rhinestones that twinkled as she walked, both perfectly tailored to her lovely body. For each suit she wore a matching cowgirl hat. She loved the children and the ministry. Along with teaching the Bible and singing, she also encouraged the young people to use their gifts in music and acting. Young people put on plays and marionette shows every week. Her other opportunities included training counselors how to teach and deal with children.

November 1956, Jack Wyrtzen wrote the following letter:

> Dear Evelyn,
>
> "How are things going these days? I sure hope you are planning to come with us next Summer. Also, would you consider coming with us full-time beginning next fall, holding children's rallies all around the eastern part of the United States under the auspices of Word of Life? We are praying about doing some television programs on film next summer, and if so, we would like to have you give seven or eight minute messages with flannel graph on the program. I would like to talk to you about this some Saturday when you are in New York."

For five years, as the "Cowgirl," she taught the Bible to Juniors at Word of Life Ranch during the summer months, and during the winter she held weeklong "Round Ups" in churches of many denominations all over the Eastern United States from Wisconsin and Canada to Florida and places in between. In addition, she held teacher-training classes to show others how to reach children. Part of her ministry was speaking at women's meetings. She enlisted the services of an artist, Mrs. Munn, in California to send illustrations painted on flannel, for her flannel graph lessons.

Mr. Schirmer asked her accompany him to Christian Business conferences, where she was on the program as a special speaker. She laughs about one incident at a CBMC conference where she was invited to speak. Because she thought she was the main speaker, she presented a long and captivating message. When she sat down, the real main speaker stood up to speak in the time that was left—only a few minutes!

Evelyn received a letter from Herb Combs, Director of Full and Abundant Life Foundation. It gives evidence of her speaking ability:

> "During the program "Word Life" Saturday evening, September 10th, I heard your testimony. Your skill in dramatics was so outstanding that I wrote to Jack Wyrtzen for your address. Your ability with a clear sharp voice; to pause in one place, while increasing tempo at another and still weave into your words a pitch of voice that fluctuates to produce a moving emphatic statement, was surely amazing. I really don't believe I have ever heard the equal to your example of this usually forgotten or undeveloped art."

God continued use the gifts of this Georgia girl, who wanted to be an actress, to teach the Word of God. Evelyn's name," Light," fitted her so well. Her happy exuberance brought light into the life of others. She was a friendly, dedicated worker for the Lord with a winning charisma that drew others to her. Children were drawn to this “Pied Piper” for the Lord. Her speaking ability captivated her audience. She had the gift of teaching, and loved to meet the needs of others.

At the end of summer in 1960, she completed her work at the Ranch just before Labor Day weekend. However, Jack Wyrtzen asked her to stay at the Inn, a conference center for adults. He wanted her to hold teacher-training classes and to broadcast a children’s story over a New York City radio station. It was about a crow that wanted to become a pigeon. It began “Caw, Caw.” That was the first time I heard her voice!

The young, unmarried people had a hot dog roast down by Schroon Lake. There she saw a man who was serving hot dogs. On her way back to the Ranch with her friend, Mary Ellen, she asked, “Did you see that man cooking hot dogs? The first time I saw him, I felt my heart go ‘pitty patty.’ I may not see that fellow again, but he surely makes my heart jump!”

Evelyn's Georgia family and her farm house. Can you spot her as a baby and a teen?

Earley & Esther Roberts, Evelyn's parents; At mission camp in Savannah; teen Friends; Audrey & Arthur Schirmer; she loved children; what a beauty; college days.

Evelyn's program poster and tract; flannel-graph lessons were her specialty; the cowgirl who loved children; Evelyn signs up for Child Evngelism with Miss Piet; best friends- Mary Ellen Mahoney and the cowgirl;Word of Life Ranch play.

Chapter 9

Surprise on the Zig-Zag Path

My heart was set on following my calling to ministry on the mission field. I was not interested in being encumbered by a romantic relationship. After Dorie and I broke off our engagement, I felt I was in no position to become involved again.

At the Word of Life Inn, we were seated family style during dinner. A gracious lady at our table seemed disturbed that I should be going to the mission field without a mate. She kept pointing out young women whom she thought might catch my eye, but I was not interested, even though she persisted.

Pastors and missionaries were invited to attend a special session at another Word of Life camp on the island. As we were seating ourselves in the grass at a natural outdoor amphitheater, I noticed a man and woman taking their places. She was strikingly beautiful. I thought "What a fortunate man he is."

Later, as I approached the conference center, I heard, "Caw! Caw!" coming from a large room at the Inn. A crowd of people was circling someone who was telling a children's story for a New York radio station. She was acting out the part of a crow that wanted to become a pigeon. She slowly turned "caw" into "coo" and imitated a crow trying to walk like a pigeon. It was the same beautiful woman. By this time I had found out that the man who had been with her was the married director of the Ranch, another Word of Life camp for juniors, and she was Evelyn Roberts, the cowgirl Bible teacher at the Ranch—and she was single!

Later I attended a meeting where she was leading a training session about how to teach children. I was captivated by her beauty—delicate heart-shaped face, framed by wavy dark brown hair, large wide, perfectly set blue-green eyes, classic straight nose and lips like rose petals. In her glittering cowgirl outfit with hat saucily perched on her perfectly groomed hair, it seemed she should have been a movie star instead of a teacher at a children's camp. Her charisma as she taught was spellbinding. People often remarked about how she looked like Liz Taylor or Audrey Hepburn. (As a young boy, I thought Liz Taylor in the movie National Velvet was the most beautiful girl I had ever seen!)

Again at the dinner table, the concerned lady made the suggestion of a girl I should be interested in. This time it was Evelyn Roberts. Mrs. "cupid" must have noticed a different reaction to her suggestion, because I discovered later that she approached Evelyn with an invitation to meet a "nice young man." Her answer was, "I'm not interested in meeting another old bachelor."

The singles at the Inn were invited to attend a doggie roast down by Schroon Lake. As we assembled to leave, I noticed the same enchanting woman among the singles. Around the fire, I volunteered to roast hot dogs for others, among whom was that lovely lady.

Toward the end of my stay, as I walked through the lobby of the Inn, I passed Evelyn who was speaking to a young girl. My heart beat a little faster as I walked by. I would have liked to take her picture with the camera I had slung over my shoulder, but I was too reserved to approach her and interrupt their conversation. But she surprised me by asking, "Can I take your picture?" "No, but can I take yours?" I countered, my heart beating a little faster, "We will have to go outside."

They followed me to a sunny spot where she posed with her hands folded in front of her, looking as proper as any queen. I took the picture. Then, fortunately, her friend had to leave. Now we were alone. I wondered if I could I ask her to come with me to a meeting about to start. "Are you going up to hear Jack Murray?" I asked. "Yes, I was headed that way." "Well, maybe we could walk there together," I said expectantly. She agreed and when we sat down together, I felt privileged to sit with this fascinating Word of Life Bible teacher. All through the meeting, I was acutely aware of her nearness. After the meeting we walked together back to the Inn. As we walked side-by-side, one of the single girls following behind us asked if she could receive counsel from each of us. We agreed to meet with her, but she never did meet with Evelyn. The weekend was almost over and that was the last I heard of Evelyn Roberts until the closing day.

"Are you going back to Pennsylvania?" asked a man who had been part of the singles. "Well," I answered, "I am planning to go to White Face Mountain first and then back to Pennsylvania." "Evelyn Roberts would like to follow someone in her car as she returns to Pennsylvania; maybe she would like to go to Whiteface with you and then follow you back to her home state." "That would be great!" I exclaimed!

I was excited by the prospect of spending time with the beautiful and famous cowgirl! The next day I met Evelyn, opened the car door for her and we were on our way! I admired how animated and vivacious she was as we traveled toward Whiteface Mountain. After parking my car, we hopped gingerly out and into our cable car seats. As the cable car carried us up, we both marveled at the view. I put my arm around the back of her seat. Later she remarked how she had felt protected when I had done so. At the end of our cable car ride, we jumped out of our seats and proceeded farther up the mountain. We sat down to indulge in the view, and spoke about the majesty of the Lord Who created all this. I pulled out my pocket Bible and we had devotions—the first time in many to follow.

THE TRIP TO PENNSYLVANIA

a time to remember

The next morning we met for the trip to Pennsylvania. My 52 Chevy was eight years old and her Pontiac was relatively new, symbolic of the way I felt about my chances with her.

As I watched her car in my rear-view mirror, I thought that I could never dream of her following me through life. Part way along, I pulled over for lunch. We had another enjoyable time chatting, but her independence came to light when she refused to allow me to pay for her food.

I purposely took a route that went by our family's vacation spot in Pennsylvania along the Loyalsock Creek. We parked our cars beside Little Bear creek, which ran down into the Loyalsock. "Would you like to see the lovely spot in the creek where our family always enjoyed our summer vacation?" I asked, hoping she would say yes. "Sure, I would love to see that," she answered with enthusiasm."

As we walked down along the stony path beside Little Bear, I held her hand. Though she was slim and graceful, her hand was surprisingly strong. We gazed over the crystal clear water of my favorite fishing and swimming creek. The sun shimmered off the water, the sky was blue and the wind blew the fragrance of the forest toward us. Everything seemed perfect. But when we returned to the car, she exclaimed, "Oh my goodness! I locked my keys in the car!" I tried to pry open a window but I had no tools. Here we were in the forest fifteen miles from the nearest town and no way to enter her car!

My parents lived in Williamsport, about twenty miles away, so we got in my car and started toward their home. Thirty minutes later, we arrived. I introduced her to my mother, who was immediately taken by my effervescent traveling companion. Evelyn called her 'Dad' in Curwensville. Fortunately, he had the numbers to have a duplicate key made. We drove together to a locksmith and gave him the numbers.

It didn't take him long to make a new key and we expected to take the key and go immediately to her car. But the locksmith would not release the key to us. A State Policeman had to receive it and take us to the car. We found the State trooper barracks in Montoursville, a town about fifteen minutes away. The trooper had to drive us those twenty miles back up to the car in his vehicle. We used the opportunity to witness to him, but he wasn't too receptive and we perceived that he was irritated that he had to make that trip. This is the first time we served together in presenting the Gospel.

After the car was unlocked, I boldly said, "Would you like to drive up to the top of the mountain? There is a fire tower there which we could climb and view the whole valley." Evelyn agreed, "That would be nice." On our way, a bear crossed in front of the car. It was great fun climbing to the top of that old fire tower. In my heart I was saying, "It has been more than I could expect to spend this extra time with Evelyn." As I grew to know her better, my attraction and first-sight love grew as well.

By this time, evening was approaching and, as we drove back to town, I suggested she stay at our house. Again that independence showed itself and she said she had a friend, Donna Smouse, living in Williamsport with whom she could stay. Hoping for a positive response, I asked, "Can I write to you?" Evelyn agreed and wrote down her address and telephone number. This encounter was more than mere chance. It was the grace of the Lord that allowed me to be with her.

At this point, though I was very taken by her, I could not hope that she would consider me to be any more than a friend.

Evelyn was full time with Word of Life, teaching the Bible to Juniors during the summer camping season and traveling all over the United States holding weeks of "Round-Ups" as the Cowgirl Bible Teacher, holding teacher training classes, women's meetings and other ministries. I was sure that she would never give up such an important ministry, and I was committed to my calling to the mission field. I was certain that our relationship would be only as friends.

CONNECTIONS

I received the following letter from Evelyn on June 8, 1960:

"Dear 656951,
No I'm really not interested in your car—just you. Now I didn't mean that for a romantic statement. It is meant for a friendly one.

It was foggy this morning, but I got home in about two hours anyway. I had a long talk with my family, got the drawings with instructions off to Munn Art so she can visualize Revelation, got my clothes unpacked, wrote to some of my most neglected friends and . . . oh yes, enjoyed part of the book of Isaiah. When I read 6:8, I thought of you. There is a good bit about the millennium reign in this book.

I saw the satellite, the plastic and aluminum one, moving in the sky tonight. Did you happen to see it?

The orange that you gave me was very good. Thought of having it put in a mold and keeping it because it was a symbol of your thoughtfulness and generosity. Thank you so very much for everything!!

Pastor William Sloat, 3300 Lycoming Creek Road will contact you about the audio records. He moved to Williamsport from Bellefonte. He is out of town for about a week. (Evelyn had suggested I contact him about selling audio records to pay off my debts.)

My shadow and I are going upstairs to my new room now. Do you know the song, "Me and my Shadow?"

Goodnight. In Him,

Evelyn

P.S. Your steadfastness in spite of all of my pretense and schemes in trying to have my own way is commendable. Your steadfastness in the Lord because of His resurrection (I Cor. 15:18) is amiable.

Eve-"Lyn"

As Evelyn followed me in her car for so many miles, she had memorized my license plate. Even though, she said it was only a friendly statement, her letter was an encouragement to pursue the friendship.

Before we parted, I had asked to see her again and she suggested a picnic. My first letter to her on September 8th was a reminder of that tentative plan. When she agreed, I spared no time in driving to Curwensville, thinking of her and remembering the time we had already spent together.

She greeted me enthusiastically and told how she had prepared fried chicken for our picnic. We found a nice spot in a forest park and soon got into a serious discussion about "election" and salvation. Earlier she had a pastor friend who was a strong election to salvation Calvinist. He had wanted to marry her, but she wasn't interested.

After the picnic, we continued our visit, sitting on a swing in the Schirmer's yard, chewing on pistachio nuts. It was so comfortable being with her.

Just as we were going to say goodbye, a young man came running by us up into the house. He happily said as he passed, "Hi Evie!" "Who could that be?" I wondered, "I hope he isn't a boyfriend." As we said goodbye, Evelyn asked a welcome question: "Will I see you again?" "Definitely!" was my enthusiastic reply. "I will give you a call, and let's keep writing."

Evelyn contacted three Methodist churches in western Pennsylvania where she had held children's meetings called "Roundups." She suggested they contact me for missionary conferences. She was well liked in these churches, and with her recommendation, they willingly invited me to minister to the youth. One was in Punxsutawney, another in Wesleyville and a third in Corry, all in Pennsylvania.

Soon, the Methodist Church in Punxsutawney invited me for their missionary conference. Punxsutawney was about 1/2 hour's drive from Curwensville. Pastor Gilliland invited Evelyn to come to the meetings to help Robbie, another Word of Life children's worker. She came almost every day. She was an encourager and supporter and was a great help at this, my first missionary conference in a Methodist church. It gave us more time to become acquainted and my love for her grew. I am sure the pastor invited her to come so we could be together and he felt like a "match-maker." He wrote in the church newspaper concerning the missionary conference: "This young man comes to us highly recommended as one who truly loves the Lord and has a real burden for missions to share with us." Again it was Evelyn's reputation in the church brought me the invitation.

On the-next-to the-last day of the meetings, she suddenly called to say she was not coming. "Oh," I thought, "she is getting less interested in our fellowship." Later, I found out that Mr. Schirmer, whom she called "Dad," was afraid that she was getting serious and told her she was "running after" that boy. She was proud and that was all it took to keep her from coming, but it dampened my spirits. She did come one last time to say goodbye and gave me a picture on which she wrote "your friend." Because she signed all her cowgirl pictures "your partner," I saw this word "friend" as an indication that she wanted to be no more than that. But we continued writing letters.

I had meetings in Tuckahoe, NY at the Tuckahoe Congregational Church. My birthday came on October 21 and I was surprised to receive five birthday cards from Evelyn. She had mailed them on different days but they all came at once. Of course that was new encouragement for me. After receiving the birthday cards, I prayed hard about what God wanted for us. "Is He leading us to minister together as husband and wife?" That seemed so unlikely in light of her full-time ministry and my direction to the mission field. As I prayed, it seemed that the Lord told me to write to her about my feelings and let Him lead from there. Here is an excerpt from my October 26 letter:

> "From the depths of my heart, Evelyn, I thank you for your prayer partnership. It's only fair for me at this point to make a confession, Evelyn. I am trusting that it won't affect our friendship. I'm beginning to hope that our friendship will turn into a lifetime partnership for Him. These are my thoughts, Evelyn. I'm not sure of His will—and least of all your thoughts. From a number of things you have said, I've felt that you don't want to be more than just friends. For this I'm willing, if it is His will, because I consider it a privilege and a gift from Him to be a prayer partner with you. But I cannot contain any longer the fact that I have never known a girl whose fellowship in Him has meant as much as yours. I wish you were here so I could say more and be sure you understand what I am saying. I really miss you and I love you."

When Evelyn received my letter, she phoned me and said: "Please don't say anything more to me about this until I see you." Thoughts of the proposal flooded her mind and kept her from concentrating on her meetings, but her response caused me to think that I should be ready for a negative answer to my proposal. I spent much time in prayer and claimed the promise in Psalm 37:4: "Delight yourself in the Lord, and He will give you the desires of your heart."

Evelyn continued with meetings in other churches: Calvary Church in Miami from Oct. 30—Nov. 4; Rifle Range Baptist Church Nov. 6-11 in Winter Haven FL. Then she traveled to Youngstown, OH, where Mrs. Swope met her. Fortunately, I had meetings in Pennsylvania at the Wesleyville United Methodist church, not far from Youngstown. "This is my opportunity," I thought, "to officially propose and get my answer."

After my meetings were over, I drove down to Youngstown to speak to Evelyn face to face about my feelings. On the way down, I prayed fervently that her answer would be "yes." I rehearsed over and over what I was going to say. My heart beat faster and my feelings welled up as I grew closer and closer to the home where she was staying. Still praying that she would say "yes," I knocked on the door of the home. She opened the door and my heart raced as I greeted her. We sat together on a love seat.

After chatting awhile, I got the courage to get to the point. I said, "Evelyn I love you with all of my heart. I have been praying for the Lord's will in this and am ready to accept your answer whatever it is. I would be so happy if the Lord should lead us to serve Him together. Will you marry me?" With bated breath, I waited for the answer. To my relief and joy, my dear Evelyn replied, "I love you too and I would be happy to marry you and serve the Lord together if He opens the way." Then I kissed her for the first time. She said, "I thought you would never get around to kissing me."

The following poem I wrote expresses what she brought into my life when I had given up on any romantic relationships and set my face like steel to go to the mission field:

I locked the doors
        And closed the windows,
Took up my pen
        To write my story.

But one window was left open,
        And in flew the bird
That changed my life
        Forever.

She flew straight to my shoulder,
        And sang in my ear,
A rapturous song
        That rang in my heart.

All the windows and doors
        Burst open and the light flooded in.
The bird and I flew out
        Into the sunshine.

Chapter 10

Putting The Lord First, Even When It Hurts

testing our faith and our love

This was a wonderful, frustrating, exciting and complicated time in our lives. We could see the Lord's hand clearly in leading us together, but he allowed problems to test our faith.

Now that our friendship had deepened into a love that came from God, and a conviction that we were to serve the Lord together, we were faced with decisions of extraordinary importance. I was committed to go to the mission field and was making arrangements again to go to language school in Costa Rica. On December 7, 1960, a month after I had proposed, the following letter came: "Yesterday we received your letter telling of your intention to come to begin study here in San Jose´ in January . . . . May the Lord bless and guide you in your final preparations for coming." At that point we thought Evelyn would follow. But problems still faced us.

Evelyn applied to Central American Mission and eagerly we waited for an answer. We raced to the mailbox every day, anticipating an invitation for Evelyn to become a missionary with CAM. We wondered about what they would require of her. "Will they appoint her directly, in light of her past training and experience, or cause her to wait until next summer's Candidate School? Wouldn't her pioneer work of starting and directing the work of Child Evangelism Fellowship in two counties in Pennsylvania qualify her for immediate appointment so we could be on our way?" One of her good friends at Word of Life, Rosemary Cox, was the daughter of Newberry Cox, who had a major say in CAM appointments. Surely this was a plus.

Evelyn and I continued to have meetings and separation was difficult. I wrote the following poem about my experience:

This day matches the feelings of my heart
While I and beloved Evelyn are apart.
It is a day from His storehouse of grace
Where light, warmth, sight and sound, sing His praise.
But each is dulled by the context now
And I will try to tell somewhat how:
"Dense clouds compel the sun to fade
Light and warmth are replaced by shade.
The gentle rain obscures my sight
And distance absorbs sounds that delight."
But when Evelyn and I are together
Regardless of conditions of weather,
Because our love's in Him, our lives abound
With spiritual light and warmth and sound.

The clouds that dull roll back from the sky
And here are some of the reasons why:
"Life is brighter when I'm with her.
God's love seems deeper and warmer.
My vision reaches farther then
And His voice sounds a sweeter AMEN."

As we waited for a reply from Central American Mission, I thought of the "Jungle Camp" that candidates go through. When I was in the camp, I had to kill a chicken, de-feather it and clean it, boil it and eat it. I was sure Evelyn would have no trouble with that for she had killed and cleaned chickens on the farm. Then there was the lessons in horse back riding—again, no problem for the "Cowgirl" who grew up riding farm horses.

Finally, the long awaited answer came. It was a shock and a disappointment. The letter from Rev. William Taylor, Director of CAM stated:

> "We are sincerely sorry that her physical condition (ulcerative colitis) is such that it is inadvisable for her to be considered for appointment. Newberry Cox very kindly shared with me your letter of February 18th, and I am much interested in how the Lord may lead you and Evelyn in the future."

Now our conviction that God had led us together was being severely tested. Evelyn feared that I might not pursue my calling to the mission field. I feared that I would have to leave without her. But we both were convinced that He had led us together. He would either heal her or bring me back from the field for some reason, but He would work it out somehow. Hadn't Evelyn heard a calling to be a missionary when she was 13 years old?

We both sought the Lord in prayer. Evelyn spoke to Dr. Charles Woodbridge, a beloved Bible teacher. His remark was: "Does he love you? Do you love him? Then he can change his field."

I had felt led to Bible Institute work. Paul Peasley, a CAM missionary I had met at a Moody Bible Institute summer course about Bible Institute work on the mission field, was planning to start a Bible Institute in Puebla, Mexico. I thought this was where the Lord was leading. However, while a student at Moody, I had worked in the afternoons for Greater Europe Mission, whose main thrust was Bible Institute work. I began to see some possibility in changing my field. Evelyn earlier had meetings in a church whose pastor, Rev. Walter Frank, was recently appointed Director of Greater Europe Mission, so he knew her. When I broached the possibility of serving in Europe, Evelyn revealed her counsel from Dr. Woodbridge. With this encouragement, we felt the Lord was leading us to approach Greater Europe Mission with the possibility of serving in Europe. The European countries had a medical system comparable or superior in quality to ours. There would not be the same threat to her health. They sent us application papers, which we hurriedly filled out, sealed with a prayer, and returned to the Chicago address.

Part of my letter to CAM Director William Taylor, reveals the intense pressure we felt at his time.

> For the past month we have been waiting to hear from GEM. Every day I postponed writing to you, expecting to hear the next day. We expected an imminent answer since I had explained that if they could not accept Evelyn, I would leave to begin language School on the first of May. I went ahead and made tentative plans with the school in San José to see if I could arrive a few days late. They said that would be all right if I notified them of my flight number. Revealing our own lack of faith concerning His leading, we both were pessimistic concerning the word we would receive from GEM."

> Adding to our pressure at this time, was a letter from Don Brugmann, which stated,

> "Our doctor's first reaction was that it would not even be wise for you to go to Europe until this is cleared up. This is because the sanitation in Europe is not what it ought to be and he feels there ought to be expert medical care until the condition is cleared up. However, he would not make a dogmatic statement one way or the other until he has further information. I suggested to him the possibility of Germany or Sweden as opposed to countries like Italy and Spain, and he seemed to feel that there could be a much better possibility of your going there.

Don Brugmann enclosed some medical forms that we were to get filled out by a doctor and returned and continued,

> "We'll act on this as soon as we hear from you and there is good possibility that if all is in order we will be able to proceed with the application and have things ready for you to meet with our Candidate School, June 11 to 18. This is all just possibilities, of course, but it does let you know something of the timing involved."

Evelyn had the medical exam and sent it in. Then we waited, somewhat impatiently, because I had booked my plane fare to Costa Rica and was enrolled to begin there in the summer. I intended to go if GEM did not accept our application or if they did not act in time. We were convinced that we must put the Lord first and allow Him to work out the rest. We prayed and waited; prayed and waited. Why did we not hear from Greater Europe Mission? Every day I descended on the mailbox but no letter was there! Waiting was tortuous. I was like a child waiting for Christmas, not knowing if I had been good or bad. But there was nothing we could do. We were thrown on the Lord, claiming His promise, "Trust in the Lord with all your heart and lean not to your own understanding. In all your ways acknowledge Him and He will direct your path." We knew that He was with us, but what was His will for the path ahead?

A portion of my letter of May 13 to Newberry Cox of the Executive Committee will reveal the testing of our faith at this time:

"Even though we felt led to inquire of the Greater Europe Mission, our faith that it was His will to serve in Europe began to waver when we approached the starting date for the Costa Rica Language School. We had agreed that should the door to Europe close, I would go on to Language School. I made arrangements to go to Costa Rica and had my reservations by plane made when we got word that Evelyn was cleared health-wise for invitation to Candidate School in June. The Lord, it seems, wanted to test us to be sure that we would be willing to part if He so led."

One week before I was to leave for Costa Rica, the awaited answer came. On May 6, 1961, we received a letter from General Director Walter Frank.

"Dear Mr. Kinzie:

We are happy to extend to you and to Miss Evelyn Roberts a formal invitation to attend our Candidate Training and Orientation Week to be held at Wheaton College Church, June 12 through 18. We plan to have a goodly number of our missionaries present at the conference as well as all of the accepted missionaries under appointment and quite a few others like you who are under consideration as candidates.

Although we felt the Lord was leading, we were still apprehensive about whether or not we would be accepted—if not, we would continue with our previous plans. We flew to the Candidate School held in Chicago from June 12-18. The fellowship was great and even the interviews with Don

Brugmann and Walter Frank were a joy. We flew home and waited again for the decision from GEM. Thoughts continued to race through our minds: "What alternative would the Lord have if we were not accepted?" I wrote to Evelyn,

> "If we are not accepted, I would have a terrific struggle concerning how I will ever be able to know the Lord's will. I told you this concerning my going to Costa Rica if GEM did not pass on your health. Sweetheart, I am so convinced that it is His will that I want to act as if our acceptance by GEM were already a fact."

On June 22, the letter from Director Frank came, welcoming us as GEM missionaries. We were ecstatic and relieved at the same time. The missionary number assigned to us was "53." Later, this number became significant.

Now I had to tell the director of Central American Mission of the change in our plans. I called him and he agreed to meet outside of a church where he was the speaker. I remember the tension as I waited for him after his evening meeting. At that time, the emphasis was on a missionary getting a specific call to a certain field. Would he understand or think I had abandoned the Lord's call to Mexico? I waited in my dark car for him to leave the church and join me. Director William H. Taylor, was very gracious and understanding, though he expressed his disappointment in my leaving CAM. We talked about the funds I had raised to serve in Mexico. It seemed an unusual move to release the money, because the non-profit status of CAM could be in jeopardy by transferring the funds.

But because I had raised the money for missionary work and it would help us on our way to Europe, he agreed to allow the money to be transferred to our account with GEM. What a relief we felt as we praised the Lord for this further confirmation of His leading!

The crisis was over—and the Lord, as usual, proved faithful.

Chapter 11

Our Forward Look

life changing steps ahead

That summer of 1961 Evelyn continued to serve as Bible Teacher at the Ranch and I was given the job as Head Counselor for the male counselors. We were extremely busy, but it was a glorious time as our wedding day approached. We were able to see each other every day for a short period, but we had one day a week off to spend together. Our usual destination was a small town, Glen Falls, where we wandered around, enjoying each other's fellowship and talking about our future plans. We didn't know how long it would take to raise additional funds necessary for us as a couple to go to Europe, but we were convinced the Lord was there already in our future.

As I looked back on the wonder of the Lord's leading in our lives, I felt that He brought us together like one magnet immediately attracted to another. During this time and down through the years, Evelyn used to sing the song from the animated Disney film "Sleeping Beauty:"

"I know you. I walked with you once upon a dream.
I know you. The gleam in your eye is so familiar a gleam.
But if I know you, you'll love me at once
The way you did once upon a dream."

I also sent a poem to Evelyn by Edwin Arnold about the wonder of our meeting:

"Somewhere there waiteth in this world of ours
for one lone soul, another lonely soul–
Each chasing each through all the weary hours
And meeting strangely at one sudden goal;
Then blend they–like green leaves with golden flowers
Into one beautiful and perfect whole–
And life's long night is ended, and the way
Lies open onward to eternal day."

We had asked Jack Wyrtzen if we could be married at the Inn where we had met and if he and Dr. Charles Woodbridge would perform the ceremony. He not only agreed, but planned to offer us an extravagant reception by changing the usual Friday night smorgasbord, with ice figures and white-capped servers, to Saturday for the wedding reception. This shows how much he thought of Evelyn to give us this special gift! How the Lord provides, not only our needs, but above our desires–more than we could ask or think!

September 3rd rolled around before we knew it. Evelyn had invited her sister Mildred to be the Matron of Honor and her friends to be Ladies in Waiting: Mary Ellen Mahoney, Carol Wharton and Mary Jane Huss. For my "team" I chose the pastor of the church to which I belonged, Sam Sprunger, to be best man. The ushers were my brother-in-law, Larry Puckett, the Director of the Ranch, Ray Carlson and my nephew by marriage, Roy Glerum. Standing in for her father, Mr. Arthur Schirmer gave Evelyn away.

Twelve-year old Paul Patton played the organ and Ken Danfelt sang the solo. Evelyn's sisters, Lola and Mildred, flew up from Georgia and Mrs. Schirmer, whom we called "Honey," was an honored presence. Attending on my side were my mother and father. (I proved my mother wrong: she used to say to me when she was concerned about my not finding someone, "If you are looking for the perfect girl, when you find her, she may not want you." I found her and she did want me!) In attendance were also my sister Harvena and her husband Jim, my sister Ruth and her husband Clayton, my niece Barbara and her husband Roy. My sister, Doris, and her husband Larry flew all the way up from Mexico with their two small children. Larry Allen, their four-year-old son was the ring bearer and 3 year-old Barbara was the flower girl.

Evelyn was a pristine princess awaiting her coronation. Again she lived up to her name "light." She was radiant. She smiled all through the preparations. It was her day! Her best friend Mary Ellen Mahoney purchased Evelyn's gorgeous wedding gown. It highlighted her classic beauty.

Our wedding was a glorious time. We sensed the Lord's presence, and it filled our hearts with joy. Not only did we pledge our love to each other, we also pledged our love to the Lord who brought us together. We took the opportunity to give our testimony and praise to the Lord for leading us together. Evelyn chose "Savior like a Shepherd lead us" to be our wedding song. It expressed our desire for Him to be first in our lives.

My beloved floated and fluttered down the path, like a white dove gliding toward me. We stood under the flower-decked arbor, while Jack Wyrtzen and Dr. Charles Woodbridge each gave a stirring challenge. After the ceremony, more than a hundred well wishers greeted us. At the end of the line, they were treated to the elaborate reception lunch Word of Life had provided.

Word of Lifers are often practical jokers. So after the wedding, we wanted to make sure there would be no "monkey business." We had a friend take us in his car to a secret spot where our car was hidden. We transferred to our car and drove to the motel we had reserved for the night. I carried Evelyn over the threshold and we were man and wife! Words cannot express the fulfillment of that night for two who had remained pure for one another. Two had become one and we were to remain soul partners for the rest of our lives.

The next morning, I found I had left the motel room door unlocked! I thanked the Lord that any mischief-makers had not found out where we were staying!

A song I liked to sing to her was "Blue Moon" by Rogers and Hart

"You saw me standing alone—without a dream in my heart,
Without a love of my own—Blue moon

You knew just what I was there for—You heard me whisper a prayer for

Someone I really could care for.

And then there suddenly appeared before me

The only one my arms will hold.

I heard someone whisper, please adore me

And when I looked to the moon, it turned to gold.

Blue moon—Now I'm no longer alone

Without a dream in my heart—Without a love of my own."

We could not use my car. During the summer, my '52 Chevy's engine was making noise so I took it to a local mechanic. His bad news: I needed an engine job to replace the piston rings. I did not have money for such an expensive job. Though I had very little auto mechanical experience, I confidently thought I could do the job myself, with the help of an instruction manual. I worked on the car at every free moment and had partly disassembled the engine. But time ran out and I could not finish the job. Even with more time, I doubt that I could have completed the repair. We left on our honeymoon with my Chevy still at Word of Life. Since I could not make it back to the camp, I asked the caretaker to dispose of it and send me my tools. I would pay any expense including towing fees. I discovered that the problem was only a noisy water pump, which I could have easily repaired. I learned a new lesson in humility!

Several friends had offered to allow us to use their vacation homes for our honeymoon, one in New England, and two in

Florida. We accepted both invitations for Florida. For our first week, we decided on Mr. and Mrs. Paul H. Johnson's condo in Fort Lauderdale. Evelyn snuggled up to me as I drove the long way down. My heart welled up with gratitude to the Lord for such a loving companion! After the trip, with several overnights on the way, we arrived in that beautiful Florida setting Saturday afternoon September 10, 1961. After unpacking and eating, we stepped out and marveled at swaying Palm trees silhouetted against a spectacular sunset. Evelyn and I stood by a canal, embracing on that summer night as we watched the beautiful view slowly fading.

I expressed my love to my beloved Evelyn in this poem: "In the Arms of Love"

In the arms of a God of infinite love,
    I have found life with purpose replete.
With the heart of a God of infinite love,
    He sent you, my dear, to make life complete.
In your arms, Beloved, my God is so real,
    For I hold His gift, the best He could give.
In your arms, my Darling, His love is revealed.
    Forever for Him and for you I'll live

Evelyn became ill on Sunday and we got medicine from the doctor. But she grew worse and had to spend two frustrating days in the hospital. Still, we did enjoy several days in Florida before we left for her home in Georgia.

There I met Evelyn's extended family and all of them gave this Yankee a big Southern hug. That is when I first experienced "hugs." I was very stiff in the beginning, but I soon got used to it. Her family was wonderful: Evelyn was one of five beautiful girls and there were three good-looking brothers. Her mother had died at age 52, but I was so happy to meet her dad, Earley Roberts, for the first time. He greeted me with his big smile and a warm embrace. As we ate the delicious southern dinner, seated around a large table, he prayed and then said, "Take out and hep yourself." That was the first of many visits to the family farm near Braselton, Georgia. We had deputation meetings lined up so our stay in Georgia was short. Churches and individuals continued to pledge support and the time rolled around quickly for us to depart.

Evelyn was an inspirational encouragement to me. The following free verse poem by her illustrates how she challenged me to be the best I could be for the Lord.

"ONE IN HIM"

"Because your heart burns with love for Him,
my heart burns with love for you.
Our relationship of soul is greater than has ever been told.
It's because of your vision for souls,
you see near and far, the young and the old.
This is the reason I have eyes for you only.
Your singleness of heart for Him makes me want you solely.

"Beautiful are the feet of them that preach the gospel
of peace"
Your footprints lead me outward to others and
upward to God.
When you hold me near and I feel your heartbeat—
I know true love when your heart beats in tune with
His—
This is 'Calvary love."
I feel secure when you're near and I feel your
heartbeat.
because I know life is ebbing away in Him and for
Him.
You've been studying His Words; not a few.
I can tell when I kiss you! Your lips are like honey
dew.
You are strong and manly. This is what every girl
wants.
It is the milk, the meat of the Word, the Bread of
Life
that makes you strong and manly and desirable to
me.
You have taken Paul's advice from Romans 12:1.
Now your body is on the altar of sacrifice.
Now it's no longer your will, but joy . . . because the
Holy Spirit fills.
You are steadfast, unmovable, like a tree,
planted by the rivers of water, and your fruit is sweet
to my taste.

Please don't let my vision be darkened or blurred . . .
Oh He is the 'Light' as revealed in His Word!
So let's walk hand in hand as we by our Savior stand. (1 John 1:7)
I have only one heart. You have only one heart.
Our hearts belong to Him.
But because you love as He loves,
you see as He sees you walk and talk as He does.
Because your very heartbeat is the heartbeat of God . . . I am yours.
We are one in Him."

What a challenging goal to attempt to live up to!!!

Chapter 12

Off to Sweden

an unexpected challenge

Greater Europe Mission had asked us if we were willing to pioneer the work in Sweden with the goal of starting a Bible Institute. After a time of prayer, we felt that was just what the Lord was leading us to do. So, instead of teaching at the German Bible Institute, we set our sights on Sweden.

I purchased five large used drums and painstakingly cleaned them out to transport our belongings by ship. We carefully packed the drums with wedding presents, books and cooking items. After hiring a U-Haul trailer, we were off to New York to board the Gripsholm liner. Evelyn's brother, Julien, brought her father from Georgia. This would be the last time she would see her dad. He died a year after we arrived in Sweden. Family and friends gathered at the dock to say goodbye. It was an emotional time. We hugged and cried and had prayer together. To think of separating from our loved ones for four years, not knowing if they would still be us when we returned, was mixed with the excitement of leaving on this adventure for the Lord. As we stood at the railing of the liner, we looked down at the people who were most dear to us waving farewell. We departed on May 1, 1962

The Gripsholm was a luxury liner and we felt like royalty as we dined on scrumptious cuisine, served by white-capped waiters. There were plenty of things to do on this eleven-day trip. I even won the table tennis tournament and received a Swedish carved wooden whale bottle opener. But we were anxious to minister, so we introduced ourselves to the captain and offered our services as a pastor and a children's teacher. The Captain provided all sorts of candies for prizes for children's meetings and arranged for me to speak at the chapel for a Sunday service where 150 people attended.

After I preached, many Finnish people came to me with tears in their eyes to say thanks for the message. They were returning from Canada where they were not happy with their new environment.

Evelyn held children's meetings in the main gathering place where dances were held. Children gathered around and sat on the floor while Evelyn presented the Gospel and taught Bible verses. Those who learned verses got to dip into her Grab Bag for delicious candies. This was the same red bag with the large letters GRAB BAG sewed on the front—a gift from a prisoner she had visited in Pennsylvania. Each child who learned a verse eagerly felt all around to find the prize reward.

Our trip took an extra day as the liner went off course to avoid an iceberg, but our excitement grew as we saw the coast of England and eventually landed in Gothenburg. We arranged for our drums to be sent to Stockholm and boarded the train to our destination.

Trains in Europe are divided into compartments. We found our seats and tried to be friendly with the other passengers. Settling back after the long trip, we began to relax but could not help gazing out of the windows to admire the countryside of our new homeland.

As our train reached Stockholm, we wondered how we would recognize the Child Evangelism missionary couple that Greater Europe Mission had arranged to meet us at the train station. The smiling faces and open arms of Bernard and Harriet Swanson removed any fear we had of not connecting with them.

Bernard and Harriet Swanson were an American couple who had served in Sweden for many years, translating and producing literature for use in Sweden and Finland. They held teacher-training courses in both countries to train young people in how to reach children. Meeting them was a special treat for Evelyn who had served with Child Evangelism for several years. Bernard and Harriet were special people, dedicated to the Lord, to their ministry and to the people of Scandinavia. They invited us to stay in their apartment, which consisted of a living room and a kitchen and a very small room where they worked on their Child Evangelism literature. We wondered how they were going to arrange things until they opened their sofa bed and said, “You are going to sleep here; we are going to a friend’s house.”

Thankful that they let us stay in their small apartment while they went out to stay with friends, I said, “We must go out to find a place to live.” Harriet’s reply was,

"You are not in America. Here in Stockholm people wait for years to find a place to live. The government is building apartments, but no building of homes is allowed because they want people to live in high rises and there aren't enough available. 85 percent of the people live in apartments regulated by the government." Bernard and Harriet suggested that we put an ad in the papers to see if someone was willing to rent to us for a short time as we settle in. I insisted: "We must find a place right away because we cannot put you out any more." "No," Harriet replied, "We all are going to prayer meeting instead!"

Because of our newspaper ad, an older single man offered to rent us a room. We stayed there for five weeks, still hoping for another response to our ad. Then a Swedish couple, going on vacation for two months, offered to rent their place on Ribbingsvägen. We managed to store our five drums in their apartment, but we longed to get settled and unpack our things.

Before we had bought a car, we decided to bicycle across busy Stockholm to visit the Swansons. Evelyn had not had much experience in riding a bike in traffic, but we attempted it anyway. As we approached their home, we had to cross the road at a point where the view was obstructed. I hurried across, but Evelyn was not aware of the danger. I called out to her, "Evelyn hurry and cross!" Alarmed, she fell off her bike and tore her good dress. She was less than happy about that! We needed better transportation.

Our transportation around Stockholm was bicycle and later bus. I purchased the best tape recorder I could find so that we would get the finest reproduction of a Swedish voice for our studies. But it was so heavy, I had to get a cart to lug it around. As we stood at a bus stop in the freezing cold weather, Evelyn shivered and was miserable. So, I decided we had to do something about that. We went to a store that made and fit lamb's wool coats. After Evelyn wore her new coat at a bus stop, she declared that it was warming up in Sweden! Swedes know how to dress for the weather.

Our apartment was over a used car sales store. We had invited the owner, Karl Erik, his girlfriend Kerstin and Evelyn's dentist, Dr. Anderson, and his wife to a Christian Businessman's banquet, KAN, where they heard the Gospel plainly given. We told Karl Erik that we wanted a good car. I had been answering ads on the phone and in my limited English asked, "Använder olja?—Does it use oil?" I always got the answer, "Nej." It seems they understood that I was not asking if the car needed oil, but if it used excess oil. All the cars we looked at were too expensive. Karl Erik seemed to like us and said he would get us a good car on the limited amount of money we could pay. We needed a car before he went to England, so he told his partner, "Get these Americans a good car while I am gone." The car he found was a worn-out Austin. It made a lot of noise, but I thought "I don't know much about cars over here." It turned out that it burned as much oil as gas! It showed how much I knew about foreign cars. When Karl Erik returned, he was furious with his partner. He then loaned us an Italian "Gogo Mobile." It was a two-cylinder, two-seat sport car. We could use it until he found the right car for us.

Our GEM Director, Walter Frank came to visit us in Stockholm and we went in our Gogo Mobile to pick him up at Arlanda airport. On the way back, Evelyn had to crawl up on the back shelf. Before we got home, the car began to lose power. It barely made it up over small crests in the road. So I stopped at a gas station to get help. The attendant laughed when he saw that one of the two piston's spark plug wires was disconnected. We were running on one cylinder!

Karl Erik finally found us a reasonably dependable car, an older Volvo. It was the first of several Volvos that we would own.

We listened to "Learn Swedish" tapes and then took private lessons in Swedish from a Berlitz teacher. We met strange new sounds like sjö for lake and ö for island, pronounced with rounded lips that never seemed to please our teacher or Harriet. It did not seem like summer in chilly Stockholm and Evelyn shook with the cold. She wrapped herself in blankets while she studied. We hurried out to a park every chance we had to sit in the sun to study. In the fall we enrolled in Swedish language courses in the University of Stockholm.

Some funny experiences came when we tried to use the new language as a literal translation from English. We went to a department store and, needing to used the toilet, asked a salesman, "Where is the bathroom?" With a surprised and quizzical look, he exclaimed, "Why would someone want to take a bath in our store? Oh, you mean the WC", (the water closet, European equivalent for toilet.) We made the mistake at times, looking people in the eye and saying "Daschund." In Swedish the word for thanks is "tak." But when we added the "s" as in thanks, it ended up as the word for Daschund.

Some Swedish young people whom we invited for breakfast thought our American cuisine strange. We served bacon, eggs and pancakes. "Pancakes for breakfast?" they exclaimed. "Pancakes with pea soup is what we serve on Thursdays for dinner!"

Evelyn and I took a 10-day trip around Sweden staying in youth hostels to learn more about our "adopted country." We learned about the different provinces, dialects, history and geography of this beautiful country and we had numerous opportunities to witness for the Lord.

Mr. Schirmer had invited Swedish Christian Business Men, KAN, to dinner when they met with the American organization CBMC. When the group returned to Sweden, two of them invited us to celebrate our first Christmas with them in Stockholm. We were privileged to spend Christmas Eve, which started at 3 PM, with Kore Ryggh and his wife. We spent Christmas Day with Hokan Croinsjöe's family. We ate Lutefisk, a traditional Swedish dish dating back to Viking times. Weeks before Christmas, the cook soaks a dried fish in lye. Then for a few weeks, she soaks it in water. It swells up and is tasty only because of the sauce that covers it. Being with Swedish families was a unique privilege and provided us with other important contacts.

Sometime later, 45 men of the American CBMC came to Sweden and met with the Swedish equivalent, KAN. Mr. McCully, father of the Ecuador martyr, Ed McCully, spoke about evangelism. Afterward, the American businessmen and their wives went out into the Streets of Stockholm to witness to the "ragarre," rough young people who roamed the streets.

Unfortunately, only one Swede dared to go out! Evelyn led three girls to the Lord, and the young people were surprisingly open to listening to the Gospel.

In September of the first year, we attended the Greater Europe Mission Conference in Rome, Italy. This was the first of the yearly meetings that were held in different countries in Europe during the first week of September, the week we were married. It provided a time for spiritual renewal, for reporting and learning about the work in other countries and for developing friendships. Royal Peck, the energetic and enthusiastic director of the Italian Bible Institute, guided us about. We gazed at the magnitude of the Colosseum, marveled at the location where Peter was supposed to have been crucified upside down and wound our ways through the catacombs. New sights, sounds and food provided an exciting first September in Europe. I bought Evelyn her first anniversary present—a cameo pin from Rome.

During the following two years, I often preached at the International Church in Stockholm. I also led a Bible study of Galatians at the Wennergren Center with a very diverse group of foreigners: students from Ethiopia, Japan, England, Scotland and other countries. The center was a foundation for scientific research and the international exchange of scientists. The students who attended the Bible study were interested in fellowship with others and some were interested because it was an English language Bible Study. This was a tremendous opportunity to make the Gospel known.

I taught from the book of Galatians and later we were teachers and house parents at a ski retreat for the International

Church. We found ourselves thrown completely on the Holy Spirit to minister among so diverse a group. When I began to teach from Galatians, a Scottish man, Dr. Neal Frazer, who was a doctor of Biology, questioned whether Paul was actually the author of the book. He had read that a liberal scholar had analyzed writings attributed to Paul and concluded that he was not the author of all the books attributed to him. I thank the Lord that I had just recently read that another scholar had put this liberal scholar's writings to the same analytical test and concluded that he had not written all the books attributed to him! I explained that the time of writing, the context and content of the letter and the recipients all play a part in the language used in a letter: a letter to my wife would use very different language than a letter to a government official. Neal saw the fallacy in the liberal scholar's argument and became interested in the study. In fact, in the course of the year he accepted Christ as his Savior. He wrote,

> "Bill and Evelyn, it was through you that I came to believe in the Lord Jesus Christ. And this weekend, at the ski retreat, the Lord has been speaking very definitely to me about what I should do for Him. I cannot continue in the job I have now, even though there is glory in writing for scientific journals attached to it. I must feel that I am serving the Lord. I am not sure that I am called to be a pastor, but I must do some kind of work where I am serving Him."

He then enrolled in Moody Bible Correspondence courses and studied diligently. The following year, he himself taught the book of Romans at the Wennergren Center!

I preached for four Sundays at the International Christian Church and Evelyn led three girls from Tanzania, Africa, to the Lord in the Sunday School class she was leading. She also taught a children's Bible club at a Baptist Church close to our home. Most of the children who came had no connection with a church. Twenty children professed to receive the Lord during her ten-week Wednesday night study.

Evelyn liked to quote from the Song of Solomon 8:14: "Come away, my lover, and be like a gazelle or like a young deer on the spice-laden mountains." I quoted that on a Valentine's day card where I wrote the following poem:

To my Love

How much do I love you?
My words cannot express;
Adjectives are too few,
And the nouns even less.
Warmth of the friendly sun,
Light freshness of a breeze,
Graceful deer on the run,
And the stately trees.
These figures all come short
Of what you mean to me:
My friend, my life: cohort,
My love you'll always be.
Your lover, Bill

We continued Swedish studies for two years. Then we attended Jakobsberg Folk High School, to study along with Swedes. In Sweden, the basic course of study in the public schools was eight years to prepare them for a trade. Those who want to attend university take four more years of academic studies. However, some who had graduated in the eight-year course, later decided they wanted to prepare for the university. Folk High Schools are designed to make them ready for higher learning. We were happy to be enrolled in this school in order to expand our vocabularies since we were exposed to a variety of subjects. It also gave an opportunity to learn about Sweden, Swedes and how the young people think. The 23 hours of class a week were an excellent way to hear and learn the language better. Our sociology teacher said that the Social Democratic Party, which had been in power for a long time, began as a party by attacking three institutions: the Church, the Crown and Capitalism.

Even though most of the students were 100% of the Social Democratic stripe, we were able to promote discussions in class about the Bible. In speech class, for a classroom discussion, Evelyn chose as her topic, "Why I believe the Bible is God's Word." I spoke on "How to Receive Everlasting Life." We were also given permission to show the Moody Science film, "Red River of Life" in Swedish to the whole student body. Of the 80 in attendance, 20 responded to an invitation to discuss the film. One girl came to us and said, "I think we three are the only Christians in the school. I often feel so lonely." But while we were at the school, Evelyn led two girls to the Lord.

We secured permission to invite the Gospel Choir to hold a meeting on the campus. It was attended by 55 of the resident students. The 25 members of the choir brought an excellent presentation of the Gospel in song and testimony. The student leader angrily closed the meeting, but the students were so impressed and interested that they invited the group to stay for coffee and rolls. Students and Christian young people formed small groups and discussed the claims of Christ until 11 PM.

At Christmas time, Evelyn was honored by being chosen to be Lucia at a school Christmas party. Traditionally, on December 13, the oldest daughter in a family dresses in white, and with candles as a crown on her head, leads other girls dressed in white to the bedroom of her parents very early in the morning. Then she serves them cookies and coffee in bed.

Sadly, during that first year, Evelyn's father, Earley Roberts, died of a heart attack. We did not have money to fly back to the funeral, but we were happy that he came to see us off when we left on the Grispholm.

Jack Wyrtzen wrote us asking if we could return for Evelyn to serve as the cowgirl Bible teacher again and for me to serve as director of the Ranch. It was a great honor to be asked by Jack, but we had to reluctantly say no. We were convinced that Lord had led us to this ministry in Sweden.

Our moving adventures that first year had an interesting twist. I am not one to see any particular significance in numbers, but the numbers 5 and 3 continued to arise. Our number with the Greater Europe Mission was 53. We had cabin 53 on the Gripsholm. Swansons lived in Apartment 3 on

5 . . . gatan. The gentleman who answered our ad in the paper had invited us to stay in a room in his apartment—3 . . . gatan, apartment 5. After five weeks, we received another offer of a place on Karlbergsvägen 53 to stay for two months while the teacher couple went on vacation.

By the time we had to leave Karlbergsvägen 53, we had the promise of another apartment on Ribbingvägen 53 in the suburb Edsberg. There the teachers were leaving to teach at North Park College in the USA for a year. But there was a week in between leaving one place and moving into another. A friend suggested we travel to Rättvik and stay in a tourist complex. We did and got room number 53! (My Social Security number also ends in 53.)

We invited young people in the Ribbingsvägen area to our home for youth meetings, where Evelyn could use her gift in reaching and teaching children. They came because they were interested in English and Americans. Sometimes we crowded 25 in our living room. They enjoyed Evelyn's stories and grabbing in the grab bag after learning a verse. Evelyn often used Erika, her dummy and sometimes I used Erik. We had made these dummies before we left for Sweden, so we tried to make them look Swedish with blue eyes and blonde hair. (Sometimes I say, "Before we met, Evelyn wanted a dummy. Now that we married, she got one!")

A Swedish friend came to interpret at the meetings, but he could not continue, so the young people coped with our Swedish and we with their English, but we got along fine. We played games and sang in Swedish and English. After a flannel graph lesson and the plan of salvation, we had hot dogs, a taffy pull or other refreshments. Nineteen made decisions for Christ and several went on with the Lord by memorizing Scripture and inviting others to the meetings. Some who made decisions could not continue to come because their parents objected. Roland Hellsten, a talented young Christian, agreed to help us by singing and speaking to the young people. One night, he led the meeting and gave an invitation for those who wanted receive the Lord to stay after the meeting. He prayed with 11 young people that night.

After several months, the time for confirmation in the local state Lutheran church had arrived and our young people were going to be confirmed. (A tradition that did not really mean much since only about 1% of Swedish people are in church on a Sunday morning.) We attended the confirmation ceremony and were surprised by the fine message by the "priest." Afterwards when we commended him, he pulled back his priestly robe to reveal a Salvation Army uniform underneath! Since the parish was short of priests, they had hired a retired Salvation Army officer to fill in. When we moved away from the neighborhood, some of the boys came with flowers to thank us and say goodbye.

During this time, Evelyn was getting experimental treatments for her colitis. While in the hospital, her roommate helped her to learn more Swedish and Evelyn led her to the Lord. Also a 15-year-old girl received the Lord during this month-long stay in the hospital.

After staying on Ribbingsvägen 53 for a year, I appealed to the housing authorities in Sollentuna, the community we were living in, to assign an apartment to us. After many trips and many interviews, they finally consented to grant us the privilege of a one room and kitchen apartment. But when the time to move had come, they gave us a two room and kitchen apartment since they had a cancellation on Flintlåsvägen. We were in our own home!

What a joy to have a place of our own! Evelyn excitedly set out to create her own lovely home, her first since we were married. Since we had no furniture, we slept on the floor and ate in the kitchen on cutting boards pulled out, with suitcases for our seats. We scoured Stockholm for furniture. I liked a wrap-around sofa, which I thought was practical for Bible studies, but Evelyn did not like the style. However, she bowed to my wishes and we paid the salesman in advance while it was being made. We made many trips to Stockholm, hoping that our sofa was there. All we got were promises that it was in the process of being made. We witnessed to the young man in charge and were even invited to his apartment to hear him play his guitar. He often jokingly said in Swedish, "Misunderstand me correctly." A day or so later, when we arrived at the store to check again, there was something amiss. Several men looked upset. We wondered what was going on. "Did you give that young man any money? How much?" It seemed our friendly salesman had been pocketing all the money instead of getting the orders filled. (And I thought that all Swedes were honest!) But the owners were honest and they immediately returned all our money. Now it was Evelyn's turn to pick out the furniture. I had to admit that her choice was much better.

Evelyn was very artistic and original in her decorations. She wanted me to create a huge frame for the collage of all of our family's pictures. She sewed a lovely frame and I purchased a glass piece that was 6 ft. by 3 ft. to place over the pictures. No one in the world had a picture frame like ours! I built a coffee table in two pieces, which fit together in various ways because two sides of each table were built at a 45-degree angle. It was so unique I considered getting a patent on it.

During our many moves, God was moving too! Not only did we study Swedish at the University of Stockholm but the Lord gave us opportunities to serve as well. Pastor Österberg, a Baptist minister, invited me to teach a Bible Study in English for Swedes. After the meetings at coffee time in their home, we had many wonderful moments of fellowship and laughter. After only a year, Evelyn spoke for the first time in Swedish to a women's group of 25.

As an American, I was invited to nine different high school classes to speak on the topic, "Churches in America." That afforded a wonderful opportunity to explain the plan of salvation in each of the 40-minute classes.

Early on we came in contact with some college young people who were eager to serve the Lord. They wanted to learn how to share the Gospel with others. So with between 10 and 18 young people, we began to meet on Saturday evenings at the YMCA for 1-1/2 hours of instruction and prayer. Then we went out two-by two to encounter people on the streets of Stockholm. Later we purchased loud speakers and held meetings on the main square in Stockholm called "Hötorget" or the hay square. On one side of the large open space was the concert hall and on the other was a large department store. After gathering a crowd by singing and testifying, the young people and we passed out small Bible portions containing the Gospel and struck up conversations with those who stopped to listen. We had put together 50 Bible verses and printed 10,000 "Little Bibles."

Once, as many as 200 or more people gathered to hear our group sing and testify. Afterwards, we stood around for 1-1/2 hours presenting the Gospel to 20 small groups. About half the crowd were teenagers who revealed a longing in their hearts for solid ground under their feet.

On one occasion, I went out alone and passed out little Bibles in the main train station in Stockholm. I came upon a Swedish soldier who was returning from a UN tour on Cyprus and offered to give him a Scripture portion with the plan of salvation on it. As usual, I explained it to him and invited him to consider Jesus. But he stood ramrod still and would not respond. After a few moments of trying to communicate, I pointed my finger at him and, wanting to shock him, said, "OK, if you go to Hell, don't blame Jesus because He died to save you and don't blame me because I told you the Way." I turned and walked away. Later, I thought, "How inappropriate of me to get angry and say such things when giving the good news about Jesus." But God can use the wrong approaches too. On my way to summer evangelism in Rättvik, I stopped for gas. I gave the attendant two tracts. He took them and said, "I met you before." "Where?" I asked surprised. "In Stockholm at the Central Station," came the reply. "Oh, you were that UN soldier. Did you think over those things I told you?" "Many times," he replied. "Have you accepted Jesus as your Savior yet?" "Not yet," he answered in a way that I saw he was considering it. So, my "wrong" method of evangelism was used of the Lord in spite of the messenger.

In 1965, we began street meetings again. Sixteen students at the Swedish Covenant Seminary indicated their interest in taking part in our street evangelism work. Those who took part the year before expressed again and again their thanks that they could get this training. They said it gave them the freedom they needed in both witnessing and preaching.

We helped in Forshaga at a Navigator's tent meeting. In addition to house-to-house visitation, we held children's meetings with 40 in attendance. Twenty children made decisions for Christ.

After we spoke several times at a "Deeper Life" conference, Evelyn had the privilege of leading two 13-year-old girls to the Lord. We received a letter from one of them, Carin, who wrote: "I have not at all regretted receiving the Lord. Today I asked a friend of mine if she wanted to receive the Lord. She said 'yes' and opened her heart to Jesus too. My best friend will have nothing to do with me now, but that doesn't matter. I can have other friends. Thank you for helping me find Jesus."

We were invited to a Stanley Jones Ashram held in Rimforsa to teach on soul-wining and devotional life. Evelyn spoke to teen-age Monika about receiving the Lord and said, "Whenever you want to receive the Lord Jesus, just tell me no matter what time of night might be." After one meeting Monika turned around and said, "I'd like to talk to you." That night was the most important in Monika's life—her spiritual birthday! She came to visit in our home several times with her friend, Sten-Eric, and they kept contact with us.

Sten-Eric gave me a book by Campbell Best as a gift. The author had been traveling around Sweden with Sten-Eric's pastor father. They held healing meetings. I was dismayed at his teaching. He claimed he could train anyone to heal. And he denied the inspiration of the New Testament letters. He also taught that when one prays, his soul can wander to the person he prays for. I found out that our friend, Pastor Österberg had invited him to come to his church later that year. I warned the pastor about his false teaching and loaned him the book. He cancelled the meeting, saying that healing is a gift and cannot be taught.

Later we got a message that Monica had died. We were so happy that she had received the Lord and was now with Him.

We were invited to hold a three-week series of meetings September 29 to October 18 for two churches on the West coast of Sweden, one in Halmstad and another in Falkenberg. Evelyn was to hold daily children's meetings and I was to conduct a series of evangelistic and teaching meetings. Unfortunately, this was the time Evelyn was in the hospital and could not travel for the meetings. Now, what were we to do? The children's meetings had already been advertised. Evelyn was the gifted children's worker, advertised as the "Cowgirl Bible teacher." How could I fill in for her and conduct the services as well? The Lord must undertake. And undertake he did! The 18 children's meetings and the 18 other meetings went well. Part of the time, Rune Bränström and Roland Hellsten accompanied me to help. There were fifty decisions for Christ. Roland and Rune led some of the children to Christ. Rune said after the meetings were over, "I have learned so much during this time. After I go to school, I think I will travel around in evangelism and take a couple of young fellows with me." This is the "Timothy method"—training others by example.

I used Eric, my dummy, in the children's meetings and once in a morning service. After the service, a man, known to be critical and legalistic, approached me and said, "That dummy is nothing to have." It seemed too close to magic for him. I responded, "God has used this dummy to win children to Christ. By the way, we had a meeting about how to win others for the Lord, and the church people then went out to witness. Where were you?"

The two churches joined the pastors of several other churches in the area to listen to Campbell Best. This was the same man whose book Sten-Eric had given me. During the meeting, I asked several penetrating questions. Suddenly, he looked at me and with agitation said, "I know you! I know who you are!" It gave me an eerie feeling and brought to mind the times demons recognized Jesus. He continued to shut me up by saying, "I will send you all my literature and when I get to Stockholm, I will meet you to answer any questions you have." He was planning a conference in Malmö at that time to teach these pastors how to heal. In spite of many efforts to reach him in Stockholm, he was never available!

CHAPTER 13

GRIEF AND JOY

John William

While we were on Ribbingsvägen 53, Evelyn became pregnant. She had an extremely difficult pregnancy. She tried to eat, but nothing would stay down. We tried everything but she was continually sick. I would feed her while she sat in a warm bath hoping to keep the food down. I bought some red wine, but it did not help, so we poured it down the drain.

After about seven months, she said, "The baby doesn't kick like he used to." We called the doctor, who had seen her only once or twice, but he said, "Don't worry, the baby will always take what he needs." We also spoke to the Lamaze doctor. His reply: "What does your doctor say?" We told him and he said, "Then listen to your doctor." We did. But Evelyn continued to suffer. During this time, she was also undergoing experimental treatment for her ulcerative colitis.

One day, seven and a half months after conception, Evelyn began to get contractions. We called the doctor and he said,

"Come in to see me in a few days." But the contractions came more and more frequently, so we jumped in the car and headed for the hospital. Traffic was terrible, and our frustration mounted as the contractions came ever more frequently. We arrived before the baby came. Two hours later, he began to exit into the cruel world. I was present and when the doctor held him up, I saw something was wrong. He looked so limp. To make him breathe, the doctor put something that looked like a bicycle horn over his mouth and it made a noise. Evelyn said: "Oh, I hear him cry!" My heart sank because I knew all was not well. The doctor, Docent Engström, rushed out of the room with the baby to try to get him to breathe. He came some time later with the sad news that he was unsuccessful. "Do you want him baptized?" he asked. "No," I replied, "He is with the Lord." An autopsy showed that there was nothing physically wrong with the baby; he was undernourished due to Evelyn's inability to hold food on her stomach. John William was born January 15, 1963.

But God had prepared us for the disappointment. He laid Romans 8:28 on my heart during devotions the week before: "In all things God works for the good of those who love Him." As I traveled to language school and someone cut me off, I said Romans 8:28 to myself. But I feel the Lord meant to help me, not for road rage, but for the loss of our first child. He also prepared Evelyn by having the Schirmers send some records with consoling songs to us before the baby was born. She was comforted by the Word of God and by those songs in the hospital. And she was able to lead her roommate to the Lord.

After the delivery, the doctor present (not our usual doctor) Docent Engström, who was a famous Swedish doctor, said, "See me in a year and we will have a fat, healthy baby for you." He knew that the only reason John William had died was due to starvation. With intravenous feedings, he would have been strong enough to breathe.

A song God used in our lives when John William went to be with the Lord was:

"My Jesus, as Thou wilt, O may Thy will be mine.
Into Thy hand of love, I would my all resign."

We held a funeral for John William and Pastor Österberg officiated. Mrs. Österberg sang "Tryggare kan ingen vara än Gud's liten barnaskara." A literal translation is "Safer can no one be than God's little children." We know the song as "More secure is no one ever than the loved ones of the Savior." The song ends with: "What He takes and what He gives us shows the Father's love so precious. We may trust His purpose wholly. 'Tis His children's welfare solely." There is a tombstone in Sweden with his name, John William Kinzie, and the verses Romans 8:28, 29.

As a result of Evelyn's difficult time after John William's birth, she had to spend time in the hospital. But it was not wasted time. She not only led two roommates to the Lord, but because almost everyone in the hospital spoke Swedish, her use of the language improved. She was allowed to go home weekends for her Bible Club and Tuesdays for her language class.

REBECCA

our miracle baby

A little over a year after John William died, Evelyn became pregnant again. And again she was constantly nauseated and could not eat. She went to see Docent Engstöm and ask him to take her as a patient. Sadly, he shook his head and told her he had no openings. When she persisted, reminding him of her last pregnancy, he said, "Wait here. Let me check my schedule." When he came back, beaming, he informed her that he could take her after all. This special favor probably saved the pregnancy, because this time Docent Engstöm admitted Evelyn to the hospital regularly for intravenous feedings. Again five weeks before the due date, Evelyn began to have contractions. We rushed to the hospital and Rebecca came into the world. She was determined to come, even after the doctor gave Evelyn medications to make the baby turn around. But she kept turning back toward the birth canal, and finally the doctor allowed her to have her way and to come into this world a 5 1/4 pound baby girl, healthy and beautiful!

I had heard a message one time about the Biblical Rebecca and how she went the extra mile (or miles) and watered all of Isaac's servant's thirsty camels. The Scottish preacher said with his brogue, "Ah, there 'tis—the beauty of the added touch." We thought this was an appropriate name for our little treasure, and a name for her to live up to. She more than fulfilled our dreams for her. We combined my name and Evelyn's to give her the middle name Bil-lyn, which she has never liked!

What a joy to come home from the hospital with that little bundle. She was so small it seemed she might break when we held her. We just thanked and praised the Lord for our little girl. But she had colic and every night she cried and cried. I remember holding her on the warmth of my stomach to ease her pain and rocking her up and down to get her to go back to sleep. All the while I thought of the many responsibilities I had the next day. After that first year, she slept better but had the habit of moving her leg to mimic the way we tried to rock her to sleep.

Friends and family sent many gifts. Jack Wyrtzen sent her a pair of little white shoes with her name printed in gold on the soles.

I wrote the following poem, "What You Mean to Me," to express my feelings for Evelyn:

How can I tell you what you mean to me
In the halting words of a man?

The thoughts reach deeper than the deepest sea,
Higher than the sky's vast span.

I can speak of the changes in my life
That your loving presence has brought.

I can speak of you, challenging wife,
Of deep lessons, your life has taught.

I wasn't so much when you married me,
And I'm still not so much today.

But you inspired me to "want to be,"
And you have helped God mold this clay.

I understand "dedication" more now,
And the meaning of "Life for Him."

I know what it means to humbly bow,
To hear your first son's funeral hymn.

I know what it means to become a "Dad,"
To be now "three" instead of "two."

I know what it means to rejoice, be glad,
In everything God brings to you.

It's not just what we've gone through together
That makes me love you as I do.

Words can't explain it, though I try forever.
It's just because God made you—YOU!

Rebecca could walk before she was one year old and loved to put on hats and long dresses. And, like all children, she was curious about everything in her new world.

Chapter 14

Open Doors

By this time new missionaries, Ed and Ulla Fuchs and Don and Liz Ritter, had come to Sweden and joined us on the team. Ed was married to Ulla, a woman from Finland of Swedish descent. They had one daughter, Rhoda. Don and Liz were from Pennsylvania and had two children, Scot and Danny.

Roland Hellsten, the handsome young Swede, who played the guitar for the street meetings, wanted to form a team to go in the summer to a resort town called Rättvik. He made contact with local churches where our group could stay and prepare meals.

Bertil, a chief cook for Sweden's radio, decided to escape the pressure for a while and bicycled to Rättvik. There he was given a Gospel tract by one of the team. Two days later, he found his way to the tent meeting, where he accepted the Lord. He remained with the team as their chief cook, filling a desperate need. During the weeks of Bible Study and participation with the team, he grew in the life of he Savior.

Every morning we had devotions for about an hour and a half and I taught the book of Romans. The young people on the team grew in the Lord, as we from different denominations, lived together, studied together, prayed together, witnessed together and sang together. We experienced the joy of functioning as the Body of Christ.

After prayer we went out to beaches, where we sang and Evelyn gave flannel graph lessons and Roland or I preached. We had meetings in front of stores and anywhere we could set up our loud speakers and hold a meeting. Although Sweden was so spiritually dead, we had more opportunity to publicly proclaim the Gospel than we had in America. Imagine Wal-Mart allowing a team to set up speakers in front of their store to sing and preach! But God opened many doors, which led to personal conversations about the Lord on the beaches, on the street, at camping places and at young people's meetings. We even went to a dance hall at intermission and had the opportunity to sing and testify! At one place, 13 children received the Lord at the tent meeting and seven at a children's home. It was a two-week missionary thrust to remember with 36 in all professing to having received the Lord! Encouraged by the results of that time, we broke into two teams the following summer, one of which, after ministry in Sweden, went to Finland to minister, where 21 made decisions for Christ.

In the fall of the third year we began an Evening Bible Institute. Thirty-two students registered to study. Some students took two or three courses but some took all six courses. This interest gave us much incentive for starting the full-time Bible Institute. For textbooks, we used the Evangelical Teacher

Training courses, which we had translated into Swedish. Since there was no book on evangelism, I wrote a book in English entitled Evangelism: Principles and Practice. Our friend, Kjell Johanson, translated it into Swedish. It was catalogued and copies placed in all the Swedish libraries, along with our Teacher Training books.

I had met Kjell at the Arlanda airport where he was serving with the fire department. Many Swedish evangelicals are conscientious objectors and choose to serve two months longer than the required time doing some kind of public service. Kjell was serving at the airport. I had been invited to teach a Bible study there. Kjell asked if I knew of a school where the Bible was taught. I told him about our school in Lamorlaye France, the European Bible Institute. Later, before we could get the Scandinavian Bible Institute started, Kjell and eight other Swedish young people applied and went to EBI to study for three years. These students would come to play an important role in our ministry.

Bob Evans, Founder and European Director of GEM told us to hold elections for a field leader and other positions. Enos and Eunice Zimmerman had just arrived with their family by now, so there were four families on the field. They had served one term in Finland but now came with their children to join us in Sweden. Although Evelyn and I had made important contacts and organized the early work, I voted for the oldest of the missionaries who had participated in the ministry. The first vote was a tie. On the second vote, I instructed Evelyn not to vote for me, because I felt that the only way I wanted to be Field Director was if all the men agreed. The older missionary was elected. Everyone seemed satisfied. But I was dismayed when he began to say that all the Swedish churches were preaching a false gospel.

One day he told us how, when he was invited to teach a Bible study at the Slavic Mission, an evangelical foreign missionary society, he presented his Calvinistic theology in such a way that the listeners were highly offended. These were friends who had endorsed our presence in Sweden. He taught that once he was saved, he could not be lost no matter what he did or how he lived. This was like waving a red flag in front of fellow believers who thought he was giving a license to sin after salvation. Unfortunately, the Swedish head of the Navigators had been recently accused of an impropriety, and had to leave the organization. The Slavic workers response was "See what that doctrine leads to."

One of the Christians, a Finnish man in the Mission, began a campaign to discredit our ministry, saying that we were a false cult. He had been in contact with some of the young people we worked with, and warned them not to have anything to do with us. Most of the young people recognized that he was super-critical, but at least one of our students dropped her class as a result. We were in Sweden to "train Europeans to evangelize Europe" and thus to work with the existing churches. Although we all believed in the security of the believer, I felt that we should not make it seem as if that were the reason for our mission in Sweden. That would be contrary to Greater Europe Mission's statement of purpose. After all, we were there to win people for Christ and to train Swedes to do the same. The Field Director also organized a trip for us to see one of the leading theologians of Sweden. At that meeting, he stated that we were there to bring Calvinistic theology to Sweden. The theologian's reply was "That won't work here in Sweden." Again, it seemed that we were defeating our own purpose.

The field leader again stated that the Swedish churches were guilty of what Paul called in Galatians 1:6-8 "a different Gospel." In 1:8 it says, "Let him be eternally condemned." To me this was taking the Scripture out of context and wrongly applying it to this situation. It was not the attitude we should have. I was convinced that Swedish Christians were part of the Body of Christ and we really differed very little in the practice of our evangelical faith.

A year later, elections were held again, as was common on the missionary fields. By this time we and another couple felt that his representing us as leader could undermine our work in the minds of Swedes. It was difficult because I considered him both a friend and a co-worker. But this time, though I hated to vote for myself, I felt compelled to do so. Finally, the winning vote was cast and I became Field Chairman. It was an emotionally charged meeting, which I hoped I would never have to experience again.

Chapter 15

Travel on the Continent

Each year the Annual Conference was held for all GEM missionaries. All the missionaries were to gather for a week of meetings, where they gave reports and testimonies of what the Lord was doing on their fields. The week always occurred over September 3rd, our anniversary. So, I bragged "I take Evelyn to a different European country for our anniversary every year!" It was also a time of refreshment as we sang and fellowshipped and made new friendships. Conferences were held in Rome, Germany, France, Belgium, Austria, Holland and Switzerland. After the first conference in Rome, the next conference was held in Switzerland. Since Evelyn was asked to lead the women's special music, we composed a song from 1 Corinthians 13.

Be patient! Be patient!
Love's answer is "be patient,"
when people are too slow . . .

when answers you would know . . .
when problems seem to grow . . .
Remember God has said,
"Love suffereth long."
Be patient!

Show kindness! Show kindness!
Love's method is "show kindness,"
when people are in need . . .
when worldlings show their greed . . .
in every little need . . .
Remember God has said,
"Love is always kind."
Show kindness!

Be generous! Be generous!
Love's attitude is "Be generous."
when others meet success . . .
when leaders count you less . . .
in every kind of stress . . .
Remember God has said,
"Love envieth not."
Be generous!

Be humble! Be humble!
Love's self-thought is "be humble,"
when honors on you rain . . .
when success you attain . . .
though others may be vain . . .

Remember God has said,
"Love is not puffed up."
Be humble!

Be courteous! Be courteous!
Love's approach is "be courteous."
    when socials you attend . . .
    when dealing with a friend . . .
    when viewpoints you defend . . .
Remember God has said,
"Love is not unseemly."
Be courteous."

Be unselfish! Be unselfish!
Love's demand is "Be unselfish,"
    when thinking of your goal . . .
    when riches you control . . .
    when pouring out your soul . . .
Remember God has said,
"Love does not seek her own."
Be unselfish!

To reach the conference, we took a two-day trip from Stockholm to Leysin, a small village high in the Alps. Our express train would take us to Lusanne and then a cable train would ascend the steep mountain to Leysin.

For days we had feverishly prepared for this trip. As new missionaries, this was only our second trip out of Sweden.

"Now we can relax", I said to Evelyn, as I settled back in my seat in the cabin. The clackety clack of the train over the rails produced a relaxing rhythm and we anticipated a time of restoration and fellowship at the conference. I began to tell Evelyn about where the train would be at various times on our trip. "We won't need our passports to get into Denmark because of an agreement the Scandinavian countries have with each another. But we will need them to cross over the border into Germany, then on to Switzerland. By the way, where did you put our passports?" With a shocked look, Evelyn replied, "I thought you had them!"

Here we were on an express train, which stopped only briefly to pick up mail at stations along the way. There was no way that we could get across the border into Germany without our passports. And our next station stop for passengers to disembark was in Copenhagen. It would take a miracle to get us out of this predicament.

"Let's pray!" we said in unison. We told the Lord how helpless we were and we knew that it was our neglect that led us into this problem. In admitting our weakness, we appealed to His power and ability to work miracles. He led us to speak to the conductor. "Can I make a quick phone call at our next stop," I asked. I wanted to call the superintendent of our apartment building to see if he could help us. "We only stop for a few minutes to pick up mail then speed on, he replied." I explained our situation and asked if I could just step off the train and run to a phone booth to make a quick call. He agreed but said, "We might have to leave without you!" Then Evelyn would be alone on the train heading to Copenhagen!

Only the Lord could work out the following details. The train stopped. I hopped off, and there, exactly where my car stopped, was a phone booth. Fortunately I had the superintendent's number and dialed, hoping he was at home. "Do you have a key to our apartment?" I hurriedly asked. He did! I told him exactly where to find our passports and asked him if he could take them to Arlanda Airport (thirty minutes away). If he put them on the next plane to Copenhagen I could pick them up at the airport. Amazingly, he agreed! I hopped back onto the train just as it was pulling out.

Now all we could do was to sit back, wait, and trust a wonder working God.

So far He had answered our prayer. The hours seemed to pass extra slowly. We arrived at Malmö and the train was loaded on a ferry to cross to Denmark. When we arrived in Copenhagen, we immediately got off and raced to the airline office, which was located near the train station.

Breathlessly I asked, "Do you have a package for William Kinzie?" "No, nothing is here for you, Sir." "When is the next plane from Stockholm to arrive?" "A plane has just landed." "How far is the airport?" "You won't have to go there. Wait here at the office and if there is a package for you, it will be sent here."

More waiting! But within an hour, our passports arrived and we breathed a sign of relief as we clutched the precious package.

We ran back to the train station, but our train had left. We explained our situation to the ticket clerk and asked, "When is the next train to our destination?" To our amazement, he said we could use our same tickets and another train would leave shortly. It would arrive only two hours behind the train we had been on. We were only two hours late for the second conference meeting. Only the Lord could cover for our neglect and work a miracle!

We enjoyed Switzerland best because the conference was high in the Alps at the Grand Hotel. We reached the hotel by a cable car that ascended the steep climb up the mountain, past vineyards, to the little village of Leysin. As we wandered up and down the hilly streets, we stopped and browsed in quaint little shops, bought gifts for our loved ones and enjoyed their special chocolates. The bells of the cows grazing on the hilly fields and the sight of the lofty mountain peaks provided unforgettable memories.

Once when the conference was in Germany, we arranged with a local travel agent to prepare our itinerary. We were to go by train to Hamburg, stay overnight in a hotel and then continue on to the conference. We did stay overnight in the hotel and proceeded to take our bags out to catch the nearby train. But the clerk in the lobby tried to detain us. He did not understand English and we did not understand German. I could not tell what he wanted but our train was about to leave. He barred the door! Knowing that we had to catch that train, I pushed him out of the way and we ran to the train. When we got home, I asked the travel agent what he was trying to say. "Did you pay the bill?" she asked. "No!" I replied, shocked to find that it was not included in our package. He was only trying to get us to pay and fortunately we did not end up in jail! Of course we sent the money to the hotel.

Since I was on the leadership team called the Coordinating Committee, I had to travel once a year to the continent. One of these trips was to Athens, Greece. The cheapest way for me to go was to purchase a package deal, which included the hotel, but I had to stay a few days longer than our meetings. Filling in the time until I could fly back to Sweden, I climbed up the hill to the Parthenon and marveled at the ancient construction. A young boy offered to polish my shoes and act as a guide. I bargained with him about the cost and gave him what I thought was the correct money, only to find out I had given him far too much!

In the evening, there was a program on Mars Hill, or the Areopagus, the famous location of Paul's speech to the Epicurean and Stoic philosophers who gathered there discussing new teachings. Paul pointed out an altar with the inscription TO AN UNKNOWN GOD. He told them the God who was unknown to them was the true God, who "made the world and everything in it and is the Lord of Heaven and earth."

I was there during the Easter season and saw hundreds of lamb carcasses hanging in the market place. I traveled across a canal and visited Corinth where Paul had met Aquila and Priscilla. My only regret was that Evelyn was not there to see the sights in Athens and Corinth and to imagine what it was like for Paul to be there.

Another of the Coordinating Committee meetings was held in Grenoble, Switzerland during the Olympics. On a break, I went out with tracts in different languages to hand out to participants. I ran into Anita, one of our eleven Swedish young people who were studying at the Greater Europe Mission Bible Institute in Paris. When I approached her, she seemed frustrated. She had been trying to hand out Russian tracts to the world famous Russian Ice Hockey team. "They refuse to take the tracts!" she exclaimed in frustration. I turned to the team that was standing around and asked, "Does anyone here speak English? A woman who was with them said, "I do." "Will you translate for me?" I asked. "Yes" was her reply. So, I began to explain the way of salvation to this famous team. Some of them said they did not believe there was a god. "The Cosmonauts when up into space and they did not see any god." We began to discuss the fact that there is really a god. And all the time we spoke, one by one of the team sidled up to Anita and tapped her on the side to receive a tract! They wanted to learn more, but fear kept them from accepting the tracts in the presence of their leaders. I trust that some of them found Jesus as Savior and Lord. And now, since the Soviet Union with its atheistic philosophy is no more, they are free to look into the matter further. In fact now in Russia, they are using the Bible in schools.

CHAPTER 16

FIRST FURLOUGH

After more than four years, it was time for our first furlough. We headed back home with our beautiful little Rebecca, one and a half years old. It was with mixed feelings that we left Sweden. We looked forward to seeing family and friends, but we were also reluctant to leave the work when everything was going so well and we could see the Lord leading the way. We were met at the airport in New York by the Schirmers and by Jack Wyrtzen. And whom do you think Rebecca ran to? You guessed right if you said the charismatic, white haired Jack Wyrtzen! We drove in Schirmer's Lincoln-continental, which seemed like a bus to us after the small cars in Europe. Cultural shock can work both ways!

Mother and Dad's place was our home base and it was great to be able to spend some time with them and with the families of my sisters Harvena and Ruth. Their father had been killed in the mines, but we loved them and considered them to be our sisters just as much as my younger sister, Doris. We also renewed ties with our other sister, Betty, Dad's daughter by his first wife. We traveled to Georgia to see Evelyn's brothers and sisters. Velma, Julien, Lola, Mildred, Earl, Demaris and Billy. When we got to Schirmer's home in Curwensville PA, we found that Mr. Schirmer had created special tree for Rebecca. He tied candies to a tree in his yard and told Rebecca to go find the candy tree. She was delighted as she pulled the candies from the tree limbs.

That year we traveled over 36,000 miles in deputation. We reported to supporting churches and individuals about what the Lord had been doing in our ministry. It was wonderful seeing all our old friends, but especially being able to spend time with our families. Our parents met Rebecca for the first time and loved that little bundle of energy.

Rebecca learned early that the phrase "That's all right" solved many problems. During that year, when we visited someone and our little two year old knocked over something by accident, the hostess would say, "That's all right." So Rebecca learned that the phrase covered a multitude of mistakes and she used it to excuse herself.

Jack Wyrtzen asked Evelyn to teach at the Ranch for several weeks during the summer. I spent six weeks at Princeton Seminary studying Hebrew, which I felt I needed in my teaching ministry. Evelyn and Rebecca joined me when I was able to housesit for a professor in a large, lovely home. It was the largest and most elegant home we would ever live in, short of Heaven. We felt like wealthy residents. Our only responsibility was to care for the house and the large yard.

My Hebrew studies were mind-boggling. I studied about 17 hours a day and had a weekly exam. One morning before an exam, I could not recall one word of Hebrew. My mind was completely exhausted. I prayed and prayed on the way to that class, and the Lord brought my memory back. I managed to get an A—as my final grade for the six weeks of study. Only the Lord could have done it.

At Christmas time, we decided to visit Doris and Larry in Mexico. They lived in a primitive village, Mecatlan, on the top of a high mountain with the Totanoc Indians.

We planned to drive to McAllen, Texas, and with the help of a missionary, Chet Bell, to cross the border and take a cheap flight to Poza Rica where Larry would meet us with his plane.

When we arrived at the airport, there was obviously something wrong. The plane was being jacked up with a car jack sitting on several timbers. It had a flat tire but they had difficulty taking the wheel off. Finally, they rushed it into town to be repaired. All this took so much time, they delayed the flight until the next morning. We had to find some way to get word to Larry who was to meet us with his plane. I believe he was contacted at his airport. Chet had dropped us off and left for prayer meeting, so we were stranded. How were we going to get back? An enterprising taxi driver tried to "take these gringos for a ride" by charging an exorbitant price. But a kindly restaurant owner offered to give us a ride and allowed us to stay in his restaurant until we could get in contact with Chet when he got home from prayer meeting.

The next morning we boarded the plane with apprehension. The plane was equipped with seats and air intakes from many different planes; some red and some blue and some green. Then the two-engine prop took off with a shudder. As it climbed into the sky, we thought of how Larry had said there were many airplane accidents in Mexico. Pilots often hated to admit an error. We prayed that this pilot knew what he was doing and thanked the Lord when we got there safely and met Larry.

We took off in Larry's plane and he landed in a cow pasture, where several men from the village met us. It was a two-hour trek up winding and slippery paths up to Mecatlan. The men had brought two horses for Evelyn and me to ride. With our hearts in our throats, we rode on narrow ridges with deep canyons on the side. Our hope was that these horses were sure-footed and would not slip over the side of the mountain. Finally we saw the happy faces of Doris, Larry Allen, Barbie and Philip. They lived in a rustic little house that Larry had built.

They escorted us around town and introduced us to some of the believers. Larry and I even got to play a basketball game! I felt like a giant among those very short Indians.

It was Christmas and to the children's delight, we had brought loads of candy, which they could not get way up there. Meeting the dear Christians in this remote spot was exhilarating, but the sight of the witch doctor and drunken villagers was not too pleasant. One Christian lady brought a chicken for Doris to cook for these newcomers. Later we heard that a newborn was named William (Guillermo) after me. For years we have vividly remembered that adventure.

BACK TO SWEDEN

the search began

The main reason we felt God had called us to Sweden was to start a Bible Institute like the others GEM had in France, Germany and Italy. During the first term I had looked for a property around Stockholm but prices were too high. So my first task was to look for a location somewhere else in the country.

Since two thirds of the people live in the southern one-third of the country, I zeroed in on that third. I wrote to real estate companies all over the southern part of Sweden. We received a number of leads, mostly of estates that were being run as hotels. Don Ritter and I began a whirlwind tour of these places.

Finally we came to a gorgeous "Herrgård" or manor house. It was where the royal daughter, Agnes, and her powerful husband, Haftor Jannson Roos, and his many servants had lived. His was one of the most powerful families in Sweden and Norway. In the past, other royalty had often stayed there. With thirty-six rooms, it was adequate, not only for classrooms, but also with accommodations for a large number of students. As we looked at the hardwood floors, crystal chandeliers, high ceilings and large rooms, I could picture it as the perfect place for our school. It was being run as a hotel so it had all the furniture, beds, linen, kitchen appliances and utensils that were needed to begin immediately. Two separate wing buildings were perfect for a boy's and a girl's dorm. There was a large, granite, food storage building with three-foot thick walls behind the main house and a three-story barn at the front of the property. Another large barn and a building with washing machines added even more value to the property. The eight acres also contained the gardener's house. Large, hundred-year-old trees ran through a long park and down to the river, Byälv, which two miles down the road ran into Vänern, the largest lake in Western Europe. The property was located only two hours from Gothenburg, two and a half hours from Oslo and four hours from Stockholm.

It seemed perfect, but one thing I felt stood in the way—it would be far too expensive for Greater Europe Mission. Nevertheless, with my heart in my mouth, I asked, "How much are you asking?" In American money it was $65,000! I could hardly believe my ears. I was overwhelmed and claimed it for our new Bible Institute. The couple that had been running it as a hotel could no longer keep it going and in repair and it was difficult to sell such a large property. The Lord gave this prize for His own purpose of training Scandinavians in the Word of God.

When the city heard that we were interested in purchasing the property, they offered to let us have the adjacent 7 acres with another house on it for $7,000. It seemed like a miracle!

A MIRACLE IN THE MAKING

I wrote immediately to Bob Barnes, who was the acting European Director that year while Director Bob Evans was in the States. He and the General Director, Walter Frank, came to see the place in the dead of winter. Several feet of snow covered the ground. It looked like a winter wonderland. Both men were impressed and recommended that we proceed.

However, in order to ensure that this was the Lord's will, several conditions were to be met before we signed on. First, we had to have $10,000 raised in a few months. We had to have all of the money by the signing time. And we had to have $1,000 a month pledged for operating expenses. To our wonder, the Lord met all of those conditions.

Don Ritter and Ed Fuchs were on furlough, but three other couples had joined us. So Merv Williams, Alf Widholm and Harvey Pankratz were with me as we joyfully and with praise in our hearts signed the papers. The property was the Lord's!

As we informed our churches and supporters in America, we called this "A Miracle in the Making." And the miracles continued to come.

The European Director and Founder of GEM and I traveled to the main Scandinavian cities to announce the start of the Scandinavian Bible Institute. We invited church leaders and pastors to an informational coffee time in each city. Stockholm, Gothenburg, Helsinki, Oslo and Copenhagen were on the agenda. Our purpose was to inform them that our school would be interdenominational and we wanted to serve all the Body of Christ in these countries.

After our meeting in Oslo, Bob and I walked downtown. We enjoyed the sights and sounds of a bustling city at night. Suddenly, a disturbance occurred a short distance from where we were standing. A car was stopped in the middle of the street with the driver's side door standing open. Then we saw two longhaired, bearded young men, beating a shorthaired man, who, apparently had been driving the car. A crowd of people was watching and seemed to enjoy the fracas. But I could not tolerate seeing two men beating one lone man, so I stepped forward and pulled one of them off the victim. With that, the unruly crowd surged towards me, and a huge young man shouted, "Don't you hurt my friend!" I replied, "If he is your friend, the police are going to take him away. I can't stand to see two men beating up on one man." I said it in English, hoping that would show that I was impartial. But another smaller young man shouted at me, "You Americans are in Vietnam attacking them and you come here to set us straight?" It looked as if the crowd was going to attack me, when another commotion caught their attention, and they moved on. Bob said, "I thought you were going to get mobbed!"

Later, I saw that same large young man, a stevedore and a student, standing on a street corner talking to two girls. I went over to them and explained that I was only trying to stop an injustice because I am a Christian. Then I told him the Gospel from a perspective I thought he, as a so-called "revolutionary," could understand. I attempted to show him what a revolutionary Christ was, but His was a spiritual revolution. He was very interested and was willing to take an address where he could take one of our correspondence courses. God used the incident for the good.

A reporter from the Oslo newspaper interviewed us and took our pictures. The evening paper of 4,000 copies had headlines on the second page saying, "An American group has come to do missionary work in Norway—America's newest mission field." We were flabbergasted at the misinterpretation! I immediately called the paper and corrected the article for the morning edition of 40,000 papers. "We are here to tell about the Scandinavian Bible Institute, a training school for all Scandinavians regardless of church affiliation. It will be 'all-Christian,' or Interdenominational. Dozens of pastors and denominations were represented at the coffee hour we held to tell of our intentions and to invite them to become a part." The morning newspaper changed the new heading to read, "New Bible Institute for the Scandinavian countries." As a result of my complaint, they rewrote the article to be more accurate, included our pictures and told about the dozens of pastors who came to the coffee. We drove from there to Copenhagen for another pastor's informational coffee.

The Swedish Pentecostal newspaper, "Dagen," published a front-page article about the opening of SBI. A large picture of Krokstad was printed on the front page. This was surprising since the leader of the Pentecostal church, Levi Petraus, did not believe in training schools, but that all training should be done as interns in the local church.

Sometime later, Mogens Larsen, a graduate of the European Bible Institute and Director of the Copenhagen Youth For Christ, invited me to speak at a Youth Rally. Though I spoke in Swedish, the 600 Danes seemed to understand. Six raised their hands to receive Christ and four others came forward.

In preparing the curriculum, I needed the help of someone who was Swedish. Kjell Johanson and his wife, Vivi-Ann, had graduated from The European Bible Institute and were working with the Baptist denomination. He willingly helped with his ideas as we prepared for the opening of the school year. Although we could not afford a full salary, he agreed to join the staff of the Scandinavian Bible Institute. He would also be part time pastor at the local Baptist church in Säffle. That was another part of the miracle. We not only wanted to start the Bible School but we also wanted to include more and more Scandinavians until it became their school. The Lord prepared the way by sending Kjell and his wife, Vivi, ahead to get their training in a Bible Institute.

The summer before the school opened, we spent many hours in preparation. Writing the curriculum, preparing lessons, arranging the library and preparing the rooms took hours of labor. Evelyn recovered some of the antique furniture, among which was a Karl Johann sofa. She also worked on the curtains. Merv Williams supervised short-term missionaries from Bethel College and eight Swedish young people in scraping and painting all of the main building.

In order to preserve the character of the mansion, I had the four missionary couples meet in front of the building to help decide on the color of paint. As is often the case when such a decision can be so subjective, we were divided, some wanting one combination of colors, others wanting another. Realizing that someone was going to be disappointed and probably would feel left out, I gave up and called in the expert in the paint store who was well versed in how an ancient building should be painted. Everyone seemed satisfied and I learned a lesson in leadership.

Rebecca and Lisa, daughter of missionaries Alf and Anne Widholm, romped and played on the grounds of this seventeen-acre property. They picked wild flowers called Blåsippor and wandered among the tall, century old trees. How excited they were to find that the local newspaper put their pictures on the front page showing them picking flowers. The community of Säffle was very supportive and the people were pleased that their historic Krokstad was going to be well-cared for.

The volunteers from the US College, Bethel, took slides of the buildings and the work they were doing. One man had put his accumulated pictures on the piano in an upper room where he was working. Later the pictures could not be found. He and others looked everywhere. Soon suspicions arose. Had someone stolen the treasured pictures? We questioned everyone including the children. All said they had not seen them. The photographer was dismayed.

Later that day, our family had to travel to Karlstad, a town about a half hour away. On the way, we again questioned Rebecca and she admitted that she wanted to look at them and took them to a little building where it was easy to see them. Because of all the feelings that were stirred up over the pictures, we turned around and headed back to Krokstad. Rebecca showed us where she had taken the slides and we sighed in relief as we found them and returned them to the owner. This is the first time I spanked Rebecca, not for taking the pictures to look at, but for lying. We had never known her to lie before. I should have instead praised her for finally telling the truth, and continued to teach my four-year-old the dangers of not telling the truth, even when it is difficult. I knew that she feared to do so, when so many were looking for the pictures.

We had prayed for twenty students to come that first year. Some thought that was far too optimistic, since the Baptist Seminary had only eighteen students in all three years of their school. Again, the miracle: God sent twenty-two students! What a thrilling sight to see the new, eager, students arriving from all over Sweden, Finland and Norway. Some were prepared for university studies, others had only completed the eight years of trade school. Courses had to be designed for both kinds of students. All classes were in Swedish except the English language classes. Many important theological and study books were in English, so we considered it important for the students to better their understanding of the English terminology.

We Americans were not well equipped to feed Swedish students, whose menu differed considerably from ours. But the Lord laid it on the heart of a lady in the nearby community of Säffle to join us. She was a cook for a nursing home but was willing to take a cut in salary to come and serve the Lord at the school. Karen was with us for many years and what a blessing she was! She served Swedish style oatmeal, meatballs, sill – a type of fish – rose-hip soup, boiled potatoes with dill, cheese with knacke bread, fil milk, similar to yogurt, bread and many kinds of pastry. We especially enjoyed oven pancakes with lingon berries. Of course, good strong Swedish coffee was always on hand. Once a year she served a dish from northern Sweden called "Sur Strömming," sour sardines, which smelled like limburger cheese. You could smell it as you entered the property!

The first assembly was breathtaking, with many voices lifted in praise to the Lord. Testimonies by several students told of how the Lord had led them to the Bible School. Daily chapel time was held halfway through the morning classes. I invited local and visiting pastors to speak at these meetings. Students spent the afternoons studying and having fellowship with their friends.

Learning to teach in our new language was challenging and sometimes funny. I was teaching the Gospel of Matthew and assigned the students to make an outline of the book. But there are two words in Swedish for outline: utkast and översikt. There is also a word for bedspread: överkast. I mixed the prefix of one word with the body of another to say in Swedish "Make a bedspread over the book of Matthew."

Many of our students had been with Operation Mobilization witnessing on the continent, which led them to see how they needed to know the Bible better. What a joy and challenge to teach these eager, motivated students! Our curriculum was typical of that of the Moody Bible Institute, with much Bible in both the Old and New Testaments, church history, evangelism, teacher training, theology, Greek and some Hebrew. Evelyn not only taught teacher training in the classroom, but also helped students with the lessons they were going to teach in local churches. Besides my duties as Bible Institute Director, I taught mostly New Testament, including beginning Greek. My book Why and How was used in teaching the course in Evangelism.

Since we could not have another child by natural birth, we decided to adopt. Wayne Detzler, a missionary in Germany, said we could probably adopt a child there. He arranged for us to meet authorities and we left for Germany. We left Rebecca at the Bible School with her good friend, King, a Shetland Sheep Dog. Mrs. Smedberg, a short term missionary, agreed to take care of Rebecca and her dog. She would not allow King to stay in the house but made him stay outside, which caused Rebecca much anxiety. She thought, "He's just a puppy and should not be left out in the dark." One morning the young dog was missing. He never returned. Earlier when I had King out for a walk, nearby residents had asked me if that were an expensive dog. Judging from their reputation, I suspect they stole and sold him. After we returned from Germany, we looked and looked for over a week, putting up signs all over the small town of Säffle. But we never saw King again.

In the meantime, we discovered that it was too difficult as American citizens living in Sweden for us to adopt a child from Germany. Our residence in a country where we were not citizens apparently was the problem.

Those years from the opening of SBI in the fall of 1969 to the end of our second furlough in June of 1971 were over before we knew it.

Chapter 17

Second Furlough

When our four years were up, we returned to America for our second furlough. Again, we looked forward to seeing family and friends, but again, we were reluctant to leave the work at SBI. The school was growing and the students were growing as well, and we loved being part of it.

It was good to be with our families and we enjoyed our time with Mother and Dad, with Mr. and Mrs. Schirmer, sisters and brothers and old friends. Evelyn and I traveled many miles visiting our supporting churches to report on the great things the Lord had done for the "Miracle in the Making." We spent time with the Schirmers and with Evelyn's family in Georgia, but Mother and Dad's home in Pennsylvania was our home base. While I looked at the beauty of the surrounding mountains, and thought of the life of Evelyn and her walk with God, I wrote this poem called :

"The Presence of my Beloved Evelyn"

As the brilliant sun sits in beauty upon the mountains,
And casts a warming glow which embraces all it touches,
Even so my Beloved dwells in loveliness among the people,
And emits a loving warmth which edifies all who are near.
As the fragrance of a summer garden fills the air
With the pleasing aroma of one of God's finest creations,
Even so the fragrance of the Lord surrounds my Beloved
And tells the world that she walks with Him."

In anticipation of our furlough, we had enrolled in Trinity Evangelical Divinity School. I wanted to brush up on my Greek and work towards a Master of Theology in the New Testament. Evelyn wanted to take Christian Education courses. We were accepted, but did not get a place to live on campus where missionaries could stay because of a misunderstanding. Our friend, Merv Williams, whom I had encouraged to hurry and apply, did get a place because he specifically stated that he was a missionary.

When we arrived at Trinity on a Labor Day weekend we found to our dismay all the motels in the area had been filled. Where would our family stay? We began to pray for a solution. Maybe if we went to the campus, we could find a place for the night. When we got there we discovered the main building on campus was locked up and the campus seemed deserted. I found a telephone and began calling for a motel again. While I was calling, Evelyn found an empty apartment, which someone had recently vacated. And then, who should we meet, but just the right persons who "just happened" to be on campus—Dean Kantzer and his wife. In about two hours, the empty apartment had enough furniture and bedding so we could eat and sleep until we could find another place, thanks to our sympathetic and understanding Dean. We found an apartment to rent in Mundelein, six miles from campus, but the apartment was not furnished. Now what would we sleep on? The Lord provided again through a Trinity student's wife, who said, "You can borrow our Japanese mats to sleep on until you can get beds." So the next day we went to garage sales to furnish the apartment. Fortunately, we were able to get all our money back when we moved out by selling the furniture.

Rebecca went to first grade in the excellent Mundelein schools. One day, coming home from school, she led one of her classmates to the Lord! Rebecca was happy to share her love for Jesus with others here in America, even as she had in Sweden.

JOSHUA

another miracle

We decided to try to adopt a child in the US. We went to the Evangelical Child Welfare in Chicago and applied. Mrs.

Hill, the lady in charge, said it was unlikely that we would be able to adopt a child in the short time we had in America, but we could attend adoption classes if we liked. We went into Chicago weekly, praying that the Lord would provide a child for us. We were asked if we would accept an African American child. Before answering, we wrote to our fellow missionaries in Sweden for advice. They thought it best not to adopt an African American child, for the child's sake, since there were none in Säffle and very few in all of Sweden. We sought the Lord's will in this and decided, "Yes, we will accept any child and leave the rest with the Lord."

One day, Mrs. Hill asked us to stay behind after the class. She excitedly said, "It's a miracle!" A mother with whom she had been working unexpectedly agreed to allow her boy to be adopted. We were overjoyed, to say the least! She said we could meet him at a foster home in two weeks. "Must we wait that long?" we asked. "I will see if I can arrange it sooner," she replied. A week later we were with Mrs. Hill at the door of the foster family. "Now, you will be known as 'Mr. and Mrs. K' and they will be known also as 'Mr. and Mrs. K,' the first initial of each of our names. When the Kimmels answered the door, Mrs. Kimmel exclaimed, "Oh, Evelyn! It's you." Evelyn had held a Bible Study in her church a few weeks before and she had met her there. So much for anonymity!

As we entered the home, down the stairs, belly first, came the most beautiful two-year-old boy! What a gift from God! After a short visit enjoying the new member of our family, we had to leave. But arrangements were made for the Kimmels to bring him to our apartment for a visit. What a joy to have him in our home for an hour. For the next visit, they let him visit with us alone. We bought him a tricycle for this momentous occasion, which I think was his two-year birthday. He was blond and had large expressive blue eyes. His cheeks were chubby and rosy and he seemed to enjoy toddling around our apartment. What a fun time we had with him, but he was somewhat reluctant to become close to me. Evelyn, with all her experience with children, was more successful in befriending him.

Then a few weeks later, his foster parents brought him to us with his suitcases of clothes. Our hearts were filled with gratitude as he moved into his new home. We wondered how it would be to leave the home he had known for a year. It took a while for me to win his confidence, but I remember chasing one another around the rooms in our small apartment. And soon, he accepted me as well as Evelyn.

After a month, according to plan, the Kimmels visited us. This was a test to see if he was attached to us. To our delight, he clung to Evelyn the entire time, as if to say, "I don't want to leave here. I like it here with my new parents." That was very satisfying to the Kimmels and to us, although it was a difficult time for the Kimmels to part with their first foster child. They had wanted to adopt him, but that was against regulations.

We found out years later that Joshua's mother was of Danish and Norwegian descent and her parents belonged to an Evangelical Free Church! He fit perfectly into the Scandinavian culture!

At Trinity, I took all the required courses and audited a number of other subjects. It was a busy but very helpful time for me to become a better teacher at SBI. I managed to get a high average that would have given me a Summa Cum Laude at graduation, but grad students did not get honored that way. I still had to work on my thesis, which I finally completed in 1980. Evelyn enjoyed her courses because she taught Christian education at SBI.

Chapter 18

Third Term in Sweden

That year In the States was extremely busy traveling to supporting churches, studying at Trinity, visiting parents and friends and welcoming our son into the family.

Returning to The Scandinavian Bible Institute presented mixed emotions. With great delight we looked forward to being with our students and missionary friends. The intimate fellowship with keen and open students was refreshing. However, we did not know what kind of turmoil we would face in light of the ongoing debate about the philosophy of our mission in Sweden. It had turned, unfortunately, into position papers and theological questions that could divide the missionaries. Emphasis on selective salvation and whether or not it was possible for just anyone to be saved was intertwined with our relationship with the existing churches in Sweden. One approach presented was to recruit students from the existing churches, then emphasize doctrines contrary to their denomination's teachings so they would be compelled to plant new churches. This seemed contrary to Greater Europe

Mission's interdenominational stance and the motto "Training Europeans to Evangelize Europe."

One missionary wrote a paper the essence of which said that the churches in Sweden were preaching "another gospel" if they did not believe in eternal security and did not teach that the only way to be saved was to be one of those elected before the foundation of the earth. I wrote a position paper stating that we and the born-again believers in Sweden were all part of the body of Christ and our goal was to train young people to evangelize their own country. Unfortunately there was an attempt to gain supporters for a certain theological position, which I felt could divide the faculty and cause great harm to our mission in Scandinavia.

After we had returned to America, we prayed about the situation and whether the Lord wanted us to return to that dissension. But He led definitely that we should return and leave the situation in His hands. The Lord had used a phrase from the Bible in the past when I was confronted with a difficult situation. Now again He seemed to say "Stand still and see the salvation of the Lord."

To our great surprise the missionary, who had been acting director in my absence, resigned from Greater Europe Mission and the conflict seemed to be resolved. Bob Evans later told me that my paper helped him see the situation and that he agreed with my conclusions.

The next four years were the most exciting, problem free and harmonious years since the start of SBI. Not only was the student body growing, but our correspondence school and extension schools were doing well. We had built a good reputation in the community and our students were actively engaged in teaching in local churches.

Because the student body was growing, we had the welcome problem of having to find places for them. We were able to restore a building that had not been occupied and to divide it into two apartments for couples. In the summer, I spent time painting the ceiling of one apartment, but had trouble getting the paint to hold. Finally, I did get the job finished. The next morning I went observe my work. To my dismay, the paint was hanging down in long strands from the ceiling. I asked the man the local paint store why my acrylic paint did not hold. With a smile on his face, he said the old building probably had lime as a covering. Paint would not hold to that surface. Now I had to scrape and scrape and apply oil-based paint to the surface. Another lesson about old buildings!

A huge barn was converted into an office for our music director and several small cubicles for music practice were built. Joe King, our music director, developed a singing group called "The Northern Lights," which toured Sweden and later the United States.

Since restrictions on building homes had been lifted, we decided that we finally would like to live in a house, rather than in an apartment. The monthly payments would be about the same, but we would have a place to entertain our students. (Evelyn had inherited about $7,000 from a distant aunt and we used that as a down payment.) We hired a local carpenter and one of our students to do most of the work. But since it was built during the summer months, we also did lot of work ourselves. We wallpapered, painted and finished the basement.

Here we could entertain students, hold Bible studies, women's meetings and children's meetings. I even built a sauna in the basement. What wonderful memories we have of sitting on the floor of our den with the fireplace burning and singing, praying and enjoying the Lord together with our Bible school students.

Rebecca started second grade in Säffle, having gone to first grade in the states.

Rebecca and Joshua found Krokstad, Säffle, and the surrounding woods a wonderful environment in which to grow up. They both were thrilled to be able to ride horses at the local stables; Rebecca began taking lessons when she was five. When she was seven, for her first solo lesson, the instructor put her on a huge horse. I stood on a balcony and looked down on my little girl on a huge horse. New sawdust had just been laid and it made the horses frisky. I held my breath as Rebecca worked to control her excited horse and my heart sank when the horse reared up and threw Rebecca to the ground. She landed in the clean sawdust and wasn't hurt. The instructor put her right back on the horse and she continued riding. One horse Rebecca especially liked was a Welsh Mountain Pony called Aramis. She called him "my horse" and could not wait to run to the stables to groom him.

Joshua loved to ride his bike and play with his friend, Björn. One day as he was riding, he turned to look back and ran into a little girl riding in front of him. He fell and broke his collarbone, but he was most concerned about whether the little girl got hurt. She was fine. They observed Joshua for several hours in the hospital to make sure there was no concussion. Rebecca's nursing heart came into play as she tended her brother. We purchased a playhouse, which the children, especially Joshua, treasured. It was red with white-framed windows and a child sized door leading to the interior. It was really like a miniature house.

About this time Joshua received the Lord at four years old. Rebecca also had been four when she made a decision for Christ.

Summers for Rebecca and Joshua were filled with fishing in the village river, swimming out on Lake Vänern and wandering in the woods, picking flowers or blueberries. Once I took Joshua to the river to teach him to cast. Vivi-Ann walked down to the river and we began to talk. While we were engaged in conversation, Joshua hooked into a fifteen-inch pike on his own. Excitedly, he called out to me, "Daddy, look!" I ran over to him and unhooked his long, flopping, prize fish—his first of many catches.

One yearly highlight for our children was the "haunted house" the students held in the large barn at Krokstad. I ventured through it and lost a contact lens in the encounter.

In the winter, our children enjoyed sledding, skating and skiing. One day we set out on a trip to the mountains to cross country ski. All four of us started out. I can still hear Evelyn giggling as she struggled to put on the huge snowsuit and large boots. When she and Joshua ran into trouble, I stayed back to help them. Joshua kept falling off his skis and had to be buckled back in them. Evelyn also fell, laughing, into a snow bank and had to be helped out. Rebecca got tired of waiting and took off on her own. I tried to catch up with her but she was far ahead. I asked other skiers if they had seen this beginning skier, but they replied that they had only seen a little French girl who was an excellent skier. “That can’t be Rebecca,” I thought and hurried on to find her.

It started to get dark and I feared that she had become lost and could not stay out in the bitter cold all night. I hurried to the ski station and told them our problem. They began to organize a search party but who should show up? You guessed it! Rebecca had found her way on the long trail all the way back to the station on her own—and she was that “excellent skier” they had passed.

One summer, we vacationed in Norway to enjoy the wooded mountains and spectacular fjords. First we spent several days high up in the mountains in a small cabin. We stayed longer than we had anticipated because Evelyn became ill. But Rebecca and Joshua enjoyed, fishing, hiking around and running from cows roaming the hills. They picked and gobbled hjortron berries (cloud berries), small, golden and unique to the highlands.

After staying in a quaint rooming house, we headed out to see a glacier. On the way up the mountain, we drove by a clear rushing stream that came from the melting glacier. Beautiful colored stones of various shapes lined the beach and every so often, Evelyn would call out, “Stop, I see some nice stones.” She had collected stones from every country we visited, but this was special. (Evelyn saw beauty in all of creation, loved to plant flowers, look for seashells and walk in the forest or at the shore.) When we arrived at the glacier we were surprised to see that it had a brilliant blue tint but was dirty. We had expected a crystalline, white mound of ice. But it was an experience to remember, climbing up on a glacier for the first time,

An old Swedish tradition was to build a huge bonfire, called a Maj Brasa or May fire, to celebrate the coming of summer. In order to serve the community of Säffle and to reach out in friendship, we invited everyone to Krokstad to see our fire and to fellowship with our students. Seven hundred people from town came. This was a time to dance around the May pole which was enjoyed by young and old alike. Some of the women and girls wore the traditional colorful folk dresses as they danced around the pole to the traditional folk songs, like "Björnen sover, björnen sover,""the bear is sleeping." Then the song changed to "Björnen kommer, björnen kommer"—"the bear is coming" and everyone tries to flee the person designated as the bear. Olle Åhlen, one of our teachers, spoke and presented the Gospel.

The day before one of May bonfires, I got a call to come to the school where Rebecca had been injured playing cricket. When I arrived, all the children and teachers had left and there sat our little Rebecca with a huge lump on her forehead. I couldn't understand why her teacher had not stayed with her. Evelyn and I felt we had to take her to the hospital in case of a concussion. She spent the night in the hospital, missing the Maj brasa, but she was soon on the mend.

A bright spot in our lives was when my mother and dad flew over to visit us. We showed them around our school, pointing out the beautiful "kakel unga" (tile ovens) which, in times past, were fired up in the day and distributed their warmth during cold winter nights. They admired the crystal glass doors and chandeliers, the antique furniture and the large rooms used for classes. We walked down to Byälv (the town river) and drove out to Duse Udde, to look over Vänern. We told them of how the Vikings came through here, leaving a rune stone at Krokstad, and crossed the lake to continue their raids on England. This was the time of year to experience Midsummer in Sweden. They enjoyed the colorful folk dancers and experienced a little of the old customs. We traveled to Selma Lagerlöf's Rotneros Park, where over one hundred statues and sculptures were scattered around on the beautiful park grounds. Some were created by the famous Carl Miles. For an added experience of Scandinavia we took a sightseeing ferry across from Sweden to Norway, and toured Oslo. Their visit was a highlight of the year for us and gave them a setting for their prayers. After several weeks, we sadly said goodbye, and drove them to Gothenburg for their plane home, not knowing if we would see Mother and Dad again. Evelyn's best friend Mary Ellen Mahoney, along with her friend, June also came later for a welcome visit.

Evelyn held women's Bible study meetings in our new home. And, as always, she gathered children to hold a Bible club to teach them. They were enthralled with her dummy, Erica, and loved to reach in the grab bag for a gift for learning a verse.

Besides teaching Teacher Training at the school, she helped students with their lessons for Bible Clubs. These clubs formed in part because of the four years of summer camp at SBI, where many children had received the Lord. Her instruction was effective in helping the students to improve their teaching skills. It was reported that there was a radical improvement in the lessons. Students who taught in local Sunday schools also wanted her help, but she was too overworked to help them with their lessons.

The Community took over the facility that the Baptist Church was renting; so the Methodists invited them to share in the services. The pastors took turns preaching every other Sunday: Communion one month was Baptist style with the people in their seats and the next Methodist style with everyone going to the altar. There was no baptismal in the church, but I had the privilege of baptizing Rebecca and Joshua in a little church at the nearby town of Åmol, a short distance from Säffle.

When Kjell went to Trinity University in America, the Baptist Church had no pastor. So I filled in the pulpit for some time. We loved those warm Swedish Christians. I wanted to help, even though my plate was already full.

During this time we began a more active outreach. We set up a tent in the town of Säffle, just a mile from SBI, in attempt to reach those who would not enter a church. Since many young people gathered on the main square, we went out to speak to them and to invite them to the meetings.

On one occasion, I spoke to an inebriated young man whose grandfather had just died. I spoke of Heaven, which he rejected. Then I told him of our son John William who was waiting in Heaven and that I was glad in a way that he had escaped the problems of this life. He was greatly offended and threatened to kill me if I was so anxious to go to Heaven. I told him I wasn't afraid, but that I wish he would come to the tent meeting to hear more about the Lord. To my surprise, he showed up that night at the meeting with another friend. He listened to the program and the message with tears in his eyes.

In cooperation with other Christians in town, our students started, "Lyktan" a coffee house for young people or anyone who would like to come to hear Christian folk music. That gave more opportunities for witness, especially to the young people of Säffle.

The town of Säffle was made very much aware of the presence of God's people when 150-200 believers from the several churches in town marched through the streets to the town square. Different Christian groups held three hours of testimony and singing on the square. Our SBI students had initiated and organized the event. How did the townspeople react to this testimony? An anonymous letter in the local paper expressed it his way: "Oh how beautiful it was when the Christians demonstrated last Saturday—stirring in its simplicity and very quiet, but not the less impressive for that. This left none of us who were there unaffected." The author continued by saying that the 'goodness' of the Christians frightens them and concluded the article, "As I said, there are many of us who belong to the 'outsiders' and long after Christian fellowship, but there is something which frightens us away."

For their Christian work assignment, eleven teams ministered in churches around Säffle and nearby towns. We were very proud to see these initiatives taken by our students.

Lars-Göran Gustafsson, organized the students to participate in "The Gideon Project." A 500-ton boat was to travel along the coast of Sweden to visit cities with the Gospel. We released the students from their classes for one week to minister. Many other non-denominational groups also participated in this faith project. The purpose was to awaken Christians to their responsibility and to engage in evangelism. Our students went before the boat's arrival to inform about its coming. Then they invited people to come on board and they passed out tracts. Several made decisions for Christ after reading some of the tracts. Others inquired about studying at SBI. Our part in the expenses of the campaign was to raise $1,700.

My responsibilities included directing the school, carrying on correspondence with Greater Europe's leaders in the US and Europe and asking American churches to pray for the school. I taught several New Testament courses each semester, arranged the chapel services and did some travel to churches in Sweden to represent the school.

I supervised a correspondence course with a pastor from Czechoslovakia. He learned a little Swedish so he could study on his own in that Communist country. He even got permission to visit us at the school. We had ten correspondence courses to offer and some of the teachers corrected papers and gave marks. Nine of the courses were based on books translated from English, the same ones we used in the Stockholm evening school. My book, "Evangelism: Principles and Practices," was used to teach the evangelism course. Swedish libraries requested a copy of these books, so we gladly sent copies to be displayed in libraries all around the country! It was a busy but glorious time.

Chapter 19

Scandinavian Leadership

From the beginning, our goal was to "work ourselves out of a job." We felt the best way for the school to function and grow in the future was to turn over the leadership to a Scandinavian who was qualified for the position. Kjell Axel Johanson, I felt, was especially qualified. He had graduated from our Bible School in France and had received a Master's Degree from Trinity College in America. He was also very internationally minded and had been invited to attend several of Billy Graham's European leaders conferences.

As our third term of service was coming to an end, I began praying about whether the Lord wanted me to leave this thriving, exciting ministry in order for a national leader to take over.

Another concern at the time was that our daughter, Rebecca, was turning twelve years of age. The moral situation in Sweden was at an abominable level. TV programs and the general permissive attitude of parents towards their children were troublesome to us.

So, after much prayer, Evelyn and I decided to tend our resignation from Greater Europe Mission. We promised to spend one year doing deputation to raise needed support of the school and to try to get our personal support transferred to the Scandinavian Bible Institute.

This decision raised concern among the leaders of GEM. Bob Evans, founder and European Director of GEM, wrote a compelling letter urging us to change our mind. GEM Director Walter Frank, also wrote expressing his concern about the future of SBI. Things were going so smoothly and the school was growing. But we had prayed and sought the leading of the Lord and we felt we had to follow that conviction, confident that the Lord would continue to cause SBI to prosper. These leaders hated to entertain our decision, but they respected the leading of the Lord. However, some of the board members, lead by Mogens Larsen of Denmark, felt that the American leadership of the school was a plus and that the school might lose its uniqueness. So after our return to the States, they appointed a fine leader to be Director—but it was not Kjell Axel Johanson. Actually Kjell was not really interested in assuming that responsibility. He preferred to spend his time teaching at SBI and pastoring the local Baptist church. The board appointed Mervyn Williams, a fine, spiritual leader. Merv was highly respected and greatly qualified for the position and I was happy for him, though disappointed that the leadership was still by a Greater Europe Mission missionary. However, we were willing to consider the Lord's leading in that important decision. And Merv did a fine job as Director!

DEPARTURE

Now it was time to prepare for our last few months in Sweden. During our years in Sweden, we had accumulated much that we felt we would need to settle in America. We prized our Swedish furniture, including a teak table that easily extended to seat 14 people and the six teak chairs that matched it. We packed them to continue to have guests for dinner and for Bible study ministries in America. Our sofa and chair, which came apart for easy transportation, would be used there also for home meetings. Evelyn packed our fine china and other treasures. My prize theological library, much of which I had lent for the school to use, could not be left behind.

A very large container was needed to carry all this across the ocean, so I set to work to construct a wooden box measuring four feet wide, eight feet long and five feet high. I lined it with plastic to keep moisture out. On the bottom, I packed all my books as a layer upon which the rest could be loaded. Feeling nostalgia with the memory brought forth by each piece of our "treasures," I spent many days in packing. Finally, as I nailed the lid on, I felt as if our decision to leave Sweden was really sealed.

This was a trying time for our children too. Rebecca faced leaving her dear horse Aramis, Krokstad, which she loved, and her Swedish friend Marianne. She spent all the time she could with Aramis, grooming him and riding him. Rebecca was born in Sweden and, except for two years of furlough, had spent her life there. She was a Swede, leaving for a foreign country.

Joshua spent his last days with his friends, riding his bike and running around Krokstad. He loved the playhouse that we had in the back yard. He was only two when he came with us. His most vivid memories were being left in Sweden.

We were leaving behind the colorful Swedish traditions, the walks in the woods, swimming in Lake Vänern, skiing in the winter and our beloved Krokstad. Most of all, we were leaving our wonderful Swedish students, so eager to learn the Word of God. What precious times we had spent with them, sitting on a dorm floor, singing with guitars and praising the Lord together. Thoughts of our friends filled our minds, Kjell and Vivi-Ann Johnson, Missionaries: the Williams, the Widholms, the Pankratzes, the Kings, the Paulsons and the Ritters. Karen, our beloved cook and the other staff members who had become a part of our lives would be left behind.

We spent time cuddling in front of the fireplace in our "gille stuga," the family room in our basement. Every day, the feeling of leaving our comfortable home life here was mixed with the thoughts of what was to come. We were leaving without any direction as to what we should do in the States. We knew that the Lord would have a ministry for us, but what? "Shall we teach or pastor or what do you want Lord?" Though we were convinced of His leading, doubts would creep in. "Are we making the right decision?" Everything was going so smoothly at the Bible School that we were not leaving a mess behind. We felt confident that the Lord would have a new director to appoint. And we were happy to leave the sexually permissive society that Sweden had become.

As we looked back over the past 14 years, we marveled at what God had done and was still doing. SBI was continuing to grow:

1969-70 22 Students
1970-71 32
1971-72 40
1972-73 50
1973-74 55
1974-75 60
1975-76 65

Graduates were serving the Lord in Scandinavia and in various parts of the world. Sören and Briten Årsjö went with Wycliffe Translators to Irian Jira and spent many years translating the New Testament into the Ama dialect. Roland Oscarsson went to India as a missionary. Others went out with Operation Mobilization as short-term missionaries; Kjell Nilsson planted several churches in the Gothenburg area. One pastor said, "The only place I will look for a youth worker is a graduate of SBI." Some students worked in their local churches as teachers, some as pastors and others as church leaders. We are thankful for the hundreds who have been trained at SBI and for the work they are doing for the Lord.

Finally, the time had come to take the box to Oslo to put onboard a ship. I hired a Volkswagen pickup and a forklift to load the huge, heavy box. It was so long that it hung over the back. I saw how it weighed down the truck, but I got in the front seat to drive it to Oslo. However, the truck tilted so much to the back that the front tires almost left the ground and would not grip the road. I gave up the idea of driving to Oslo and drove to a local cargo company to transport the box. What a relief not to have attempted the three-hour drive in such a loaded vehicle!

After the truck was unloaded, I picked up our playhouse to take it to Krokstad. I did not realize that Joshua had wanted to go along to see his beloved playhouse delivered. I hopped in the truck and started off, not knowing that Joshua was frantically speeding his bike down the road to go along. Neither did I hear Evelyn shouting, "Wait for Joshua!" This was heartbreaking for Josh and he still remembers the trauma he experienced.

My heart melted – finally we met; beautiful bride; that transfixing gaze; wedding vows; happy to feed me; Word of Life reception; honeymoon; looking to the future.

A Pristine Princess

Bound for Sweden- packing and loading; Evelyn with her Dad; together on the Gripsholm; a big turnout- farewell to family and friends; treated like royalty.

Evelyn and newborn Rebecca; our new family; proud mamma; "Oh, hi!"; Kinzie family portrait.

KROKSTAD MANOR BECOMES G.E.M. PROPERTY

February 3, 1969 became a significant date in the history of the Scandinavian Bible Institute when Swedish Field Director, Bill Kinzie, signed for the new property at Saffle, Sweden. Fellow missionaries Mervyn Williams, Alf Widholm and Harvey Pankratz were present for the historic occasion.

Krokstad – Christian service is part of training; the student body grows.

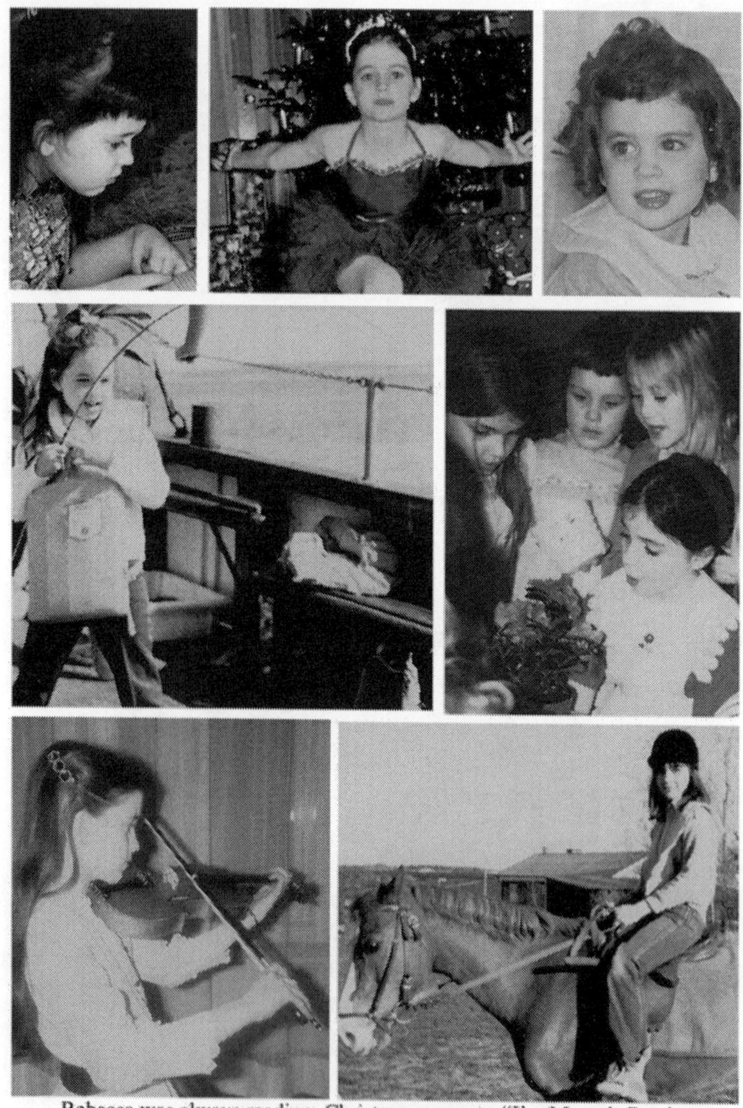

Rebecca was always reading; Christmas presents; "I'm Mama's Precious Darling;"deep sea fishing; birthday fun; violin recital; riding lessons.

Fishing in Norway; Joshua and Rebecca; returning to Sweden; a visit with my mother in Barbours, PA; playing in the sand; Christmas presents from America.

Joshua and Evelyn at Krokstad; Josh loved that hammer; happy birthday; what a cutie; playing in the mud; Joshua's favorite bear.

Chapter 20

On the Way Home

A leather covered Bible published in 1822 tells of how our ancestor, Alexander MacKenzie, came with his second wife and six children to America in 1774. For some reason the name was changed to Kinzie, which name all of his children assumed. I wanted to see my ancestor's land and visit the MacKenzie castle. So on our way back to the States, we decided to tour England and Scotland.

We flew to London, did some sightseeing and then flew on to Glasgow. There we rented a VW van to tour Scotland. It was June but the salesman wanted to rent us four sleeping bags for the cold we should encounter. I thought the price was too high and that we would not really need them in the Summer. How wrong I was! Our children could not sleep in the hammocks that were situated above our heads in the van. The cold came right up through to them. So we slept side-by-side, diagonally because of my height. As soon as we could, we purchased heavy jackets and two sheep skin rugs!

It was exciting to visit Edinburg and then to arrive at the MacKenzie castle, called Eilean Donan castle after the caretakers. Inside a guide told us an amusing legend. He said that the MacKenzies and the MacDonalds were always feuding. The MacDonalds lived across the waters of Loch Duich on the Isle of Skye. However, the MacKenzie chief married the MacDonald chief's daughter to make peace. On one occasion, the MacKenzie chief visited the Isle, but being too proud to be on MacDonald property, purchased the plot of land he was staying on. A fight broke out at a drunken party he attended and he was thrown off the island. In a fit of rage, he tried to get even. His wife happened to be cross-eyed. So he sent her back to the Isle of Skye on a one eyed donkey led by a cross eyed servant. That started another battle between the MacKenzies and MacDonalds!

We had an exciting time when we left Glasgow. Our plane had come from London to Glasgow. The company from which we rented the Volkswagen RV agreed to pick us up and then take us back to the airport. We didn't realize that there were two airports in Glasgow and he took us to the one we had come in on. The other airport was the international airport. When we arrived there, we were informed, to our surprise, that we needed to go to the other airport, but we could not get there in time to catch our plane! Amazingly, the airline sent us back to London and put us up in a hotel, free of charge! In spite our error, the Lord found a way. We took off the next morning for our home country.

We needed guidance from the Lord in this new step of faith. We had committed the coming year to representing the Scandinavian Bible Institute and attempting to raise support—especially from the churches that had supported us. But after that year, we did not know how the Lord would lead us.

As we looked back over the past years, I wrote the following expression of His leading to this point called, "Adventure in Faith."

A blossoming flower, my wife to be
　　An eternal rose she is to me.
Left home and country to serve the Lord
　　Loving Jesus and carrying His Word.
We met at a lake around a fire.
　　She soon became my heart's desire.
Whiteface mountain, our first date.
　　My proposal of marriage was not too late.
"Yes," she said, "We've a calling to fulfill."
　　"We'll live our lives according to His will.
Off to Sweden we went to start a school.
　　It only could happen if we were His tools.
By faith we asked Him our path to lead.
　　He alone must do it for us to succeed.
Bright young people soon came our way.
　　"Teach us to witness and what to say."
God opened the door in the main part of town.
　　Going out by faith, we set our speakers down,
And sang and spoke of the Lord we love.
　　Depending on the Spirit for help from above.

We studied the language at University,
Learning the language, a necessity.
Evening Bible School soon came to be.
The Word could be taught open and free.
This led to the miracle of a beautiful place
To teach the Word and witness His grace.
Krokstad Manor house with sixty rooms,
Opened to us like butterfly cocoons.
No time could tell all the wonders He did
As His promises in our hearts we hid.
Students from all Scandinavia came,
To learn His Word and praise His name.
God blessed us with children along the path:
John William, too weak to breathe at birth.
Miracle Rebecca came to bless our home.
Two-year old Joshua came to set the tone.
Sweet fellowship we had as we sang and prayed.
A burden for lost people on our hearts was laid.
Years of teaching and graduates went
To spread the Word, from here to Orient.
Another ministry for us to come,
We left the field and went on home.
It amazes us yet that God could use,
Ordinary people as He does choose.

We decided to settle for the time being in Lancaster, PA. Since I had to travel back to New York to get our belongings, which had been shipped ahead of us, I rented a pick-up truck. Unfortunately, a severe rainstorm came up and drenched the large wooden box where my library books were stored. The books got wet but we were able to salvage most of them.

We purchased a home in Lancaster, PA and were given financial help in buying furniture by the Presbyterian Church of Coatesville, PA. Rebecca prepared a May Pole and we invited the people from the church for a party.

Since it was the Bicentennial celebration and we felt our children had to get oriented to America and history they had not learned in Sweden, we traveled to Philadelphia, Washington, Mt. Vernon, and Williamsburg, VA. We saw the replicas of Columbus' ships and other sights new to our children. It was a time of orientation for them but Rebecca was very homesick and experiencing culture shock. She didn't feel comfortable in American culture and missed everything about Sweden, especially Aramis and Krokstad. She was so miserable that she would wake up vomiting several times a month. We enrolled Joshua and Rebecca in a Christian School and settled in our new home.

During this year of travel, I also worked on my ThM thesis. Towards the end of the year, I applied for a teaching position at Lancaster Bible College. My interview went very well and they seemed ready to accept me. However, they asked a question that I could not answer to their satisfaction. I was asked to commit myself to saying that the gift of tongues had ceased and anything to the contrary is of the devil. Their position was based on 1 Corinthians 13 which said "tongues shall cease." Since the same passage said that "knowledge shall cease," I felt that I could not say uncategorically that God could not use that gift if He wants. But I said, "I see no need for that gift today since we have the Word of God and the Holy Spirit as our Teacher. I totally disagree with the Pentecostals who say that everyone must speak in tongues to be spiritual. That is false teaching and is not in accord with the Word of God. Much, if not all of that ecstatic speaking, I believe, is self delusion."

Because I could not say that God cannot use tongues under any circumstance, they would not accept me as a teacher. I had to interpret 1 Corinthians 13 as they did to be a teacher at LBI. So, God closed that door.

During this time, we had the privilege of having Kjell, Vivi, Inger and Märta live with us in Lancaster, while he did Biblical research with the view of starting a fourth graduate year at SBI.

Toward the end of that year, I had a speaking engagement at a large church in Allentown, PA. After the service, I was surprised when a man, surrounded by several people, asked if they could see me in a back room. I agreed and they asked if I were interested in candidating for pastor of their church, Memorial Baptist Church in Williamsport, PA. It appeared that this might be the open door the Lord was setting before us, so I agreed to an interview.

They put our family up in a motel overlooking the International Little League baseball field. The next day I met with the deacons of the church. It was a very cordial interview. But at one point, I was asked my opinion of Billy Graham. I said I was very happy that he is preaching and people are coming to Christ. "But would you support him if he held a campaign in Williamsport?" "Of course," I answered, "I want to see people come to Christ." Although that answer did not please them, one leader responded, "It is not likely that he will come to Williamsport." With that, they decided to put it to a vote before the congregation. The final vote was something like 190 for and 6 against. When the letter came of the vote, I felt that it was a wide enough margin, though I had hoped for a 100% vote. We answered the call with a "yes" and we began preparations to move to Williamsport.

Memorial Baptist had a 140 year-old history. It was originally called "Second Baptist Church." But on December 24, 1872 at a Christmas tree party on the second floor, a tragedy had occurred. The floor collapsed plunging the gathered congregation to the wreckage of the floor below. Thirteen people were killed and 48 injured. The church was quickly rebuilt and renamed "Memorial Baptist Church." A new building was dedicated in 1910 and a large educational building added in 1966, 11 years before we arrived.

A fine reception was arranged for us. But I was confronted with some of the problems I was to inherit from the previous pastor, a Bob Jones graduate. The church was in turmoil. One Sunday he announced that he was resigning. The next Sunday he said he took back his resignation, but the people would not accept him back. He left a rather legalistic spirit behind. Some of the women of the church asked if I thought it was sinful to wear slacks! "God looks on the inside, not on your clothing!" I replied. My ministry was set out for me: to have a spiritually and emotionally healing ministry, to teach about loving each other as brothers, to emphasize the freedom from legalism we have in Christ, and showing that the Lord's first desire is a personal fellowship with Him.

Rebecca and Joshua began in the public school system. Joshua struggled in school and was later diagnosed with dyslexia. Our children then attended a Christian School that used the self-study method of teaching. Rebecca did well and Joshua caught up to his grade level. But we felt a little uncomfortable because the church, which ran the school, was Pentecostal.

We became close friends with Sandy and Charles Westgate, pastor of Community Baptist Church, one of our missionary supporting churches. He was the one who had sent my resume to Memorial when they were looking for pastor.

When the Williamsport High School began teaching about all kinds of sex perversion, we joined other pastors in the area to object. We were not opposed to the biological teaching of sex, but when they planed to include sex perversions without any moral compass, we were dismayed. The school board would not even give us a hearing. As a result, we and several other pastors of different denominations decided to start a Christian school that was neither hyper legalistic nor Pentecostal. Several other churches joined in to offer a more Biblical curriculum and atmosphere. We purchased a large building and school began. Rebecca and Joshua attended until we left Williamsport.

I preached every Sunday morning and evening and had the midweek Bible Study. In my preaching, I felt it necessary to preach on love and harmony in the church as a part of the Christian life. But the Gospel was also a part of every sermon and I gave an invitation at the close of the morning service. However, it seemed that more people came to Christ as a result of my hospital visits. Memorial had an active membership of about 500 and an inactive membership of about 500. Consequently, both active and inactive members called on me. I visited in each of the two hospitals at least once a week. Sometimes Rebecca liked to go with me to visit.

There were a number who trusted Christ as Savior, but I especially remember one lady. She said she did not believe there was a God. Because she was slowly dying, I visited her often and gradually she accepted Christ and the peace He gives. She died a short time later.

I felt that the Lord began healing the church of the strife that was left after the departure of the former pastor. A new sense of cooperation and harmony began to develop.

As a part of my ministry I emphasized the training of the Deacons to take leadership in the worship services. They had a little experience in leading while they were looking for a pastor. Previously, pastors led the entire service. I insisted that they lead reading the Bible, praying and making the announcements. Some were reluctant, but all complied and got better as time went on.

I held several classes to teach members how to lead a person to Christ. After several sessions, I asked the class to come one night to team up two by two to visit in homes. Only two couples and a man showed up! Personal evangelism was not easy when it came down to the idea of visitation. But that one man, Charlie, and I teamed up for the entire time we were at Memorial to do home visitation.

Fred Plocinski continued to question and reject the Gospel. His wife was a Christian and was very concerned about him. I spent many hours witnessing to him in his home, but he was resistant. One Sunday evening he came to church when we were showing a film about the second coming of Christ. After the service, one of his young sons asked why he would not be in Heaven with him. That broke through to his heart and he accepted Christ. Later, after some growth, he became a fine leader in the church.

One of the highlights of our four years at Memorial was a Word of Life Rally, with the 100 voice Word of Life Choral performing. Jack Wyrtzen, founder and director of Word of Life, and Harry Bollback led the meeting. Reservations filled so rapidly that we had to announce in the paper that they were filled. Every seat was taken with over 700 in attendance. Since Evelyn had been the Bible teacher at the Ranch every summer and traveled all over the States holding children's and women's meetings and teacher training classes for WOL, Jack's presence was a special blessing to us. The church went all out to provide a fine reception in the recreation hall. Evelyn walked around singing her theme song as WOL teacher: "I want to be a rancher for my Savior," to the delight of the Word of Lifers. In order to try to get into the WOL spirit of fun, I tapped my glass for attention and addressed Jack. I knew how much Evelyn's ministry meant to Word of Life and how Jack missed her ministry, so I turned to Jack and said: "Jack, I want to apologize for taking Evelyn from Word of Life." To my dismay, everyone took it wrongly and broke out in laughter, interpreting it to mean that I should have left Evelyn there! I was thoroughly embarrassed!

Evelyn formed a children's choir, entertained in our home, did visitation and worked with the ladies of the church. Although Evelyn is an excellent teacher, all Sunday School positions were taken, so she substituted when asked. It seemed that her exceptional gifts in teaching were not being used. But, as she usually did everywhere she lived, she started a children's Bible club and a women's Bible study.

Some things about Memorial were frustrating. The Missions Committee held all the power of who was to be supported. Although Kjell and Vivi-Ann, our dear friends from Sweden, spent several weeks with us and preached for me one Sunday, there was no interest in adding them to the missionary budget. About half of the Church's income each year went out to support missionaries. We were happy that about $50,000 was given for missions, but none for Sweden or Kjell and Vivi. The committee had their favorites whose salaries they increased rather than adding new missionaries. Our friend, Charlie, did send some monthly support for Kjell and Vivi.

There was other evidence of the controlling atmosphere in the church. The paid organist led a sewing circle. Evelyn approached her to ask, "May I join your sewing circle? I would like to get better acquainted with some of the ladies of the church?" The answer was, "No, there is no more room in our circle." Even the pastor's wife was excluded! She was expected to be the "honorary pastor's wife."

But Evelyn found a way to minister. She started a children's choir and a home Bible study for women and a children's club. I had Rebecca and Evelyn frequently sing duets at the morning worship. Evelyn often spent the Sunday School hour visiting people who were not in any church to invite them to join us. Evelyn was called to an active ministry when she was 13 and always found a way to serve.

Even though there was a spirit of "we have always done it this way," we did have a good time of ministry at Memorial. We loved the people and were well loved. Some said we were the best pastor's couple they have had. Lasting friendships were made and the people appreciated our ministry. Although the exhortation in some of my messages might have seemed a little harsh, we were not aware of any criticism. We felt loved and appreciated, but we longed to be involved in a more pioneer type of work—probably church planting.

CHAPTER 21

A New Ministry

We felt the Lord leading us by faith into a new ministry after four years at Memorial. I had finished the work on my ThM (masters in New Testament) thesis and had to travel to Trinity Evangelical Divinity School to defend it. We decided that I would combine the trip with an excursion to other cities where there was a need for new churches. San Antonio, TX was one of the places. It was growing rapidly and we felt it was an ideal place to plant a church. I wrote to Pastor Steve Troxel, of Wayside Chapel, an Evangelical Free Church with a membership of about 1,000. He encouraged me to come and meet with his elders because they were interested in helping plant a new church. At the meeting with the elders, they asked me to come to be a part of their church for six months before they would talk about planting a new church. But I did not feel led to put off the ministry to which we were called.

Up to this point, the church was not aware of our plans. At a Palm Sunday morning service, we announced our resignation and told of the new ministry the Lord had laid on our heart. It was a step of faith, for at that time, we had no financial support for this new ministry. We would have to depend upon savings at the beginning.

An interesting sidelight was that our friends, Dave and Faye Walz, came forward the same morning we announced our resignation to take a new step of faith to serve with a Jewish Mission.

We stayed on to minister through August. During that time, we flew to San Antonio to look for a house. We were whisked from one house to another until we settled on a ranch style in Northeast San Antonio. It was a new housing development and was close to both a high school and an elementary school.

On August 15, 1981, there was a tearful and appreciative going-away reception with the dear friends of our congregation. They took up a welcome love offering to help us in this step of faith. The church also took us on for $300 a month support. This was especially impressive since we were not going to plant a Baptist church but an Evangelical Free church. In one way, we hated to leave after seeing the Lord work at and through Memorial Baptist Church. Even though it was difficult to depart, we felt sure that the Lord wanted us in a more missionary type of ministry. So in faith that the Lord was leading the way, we said goodbye to four years of ministry and to dear friends at Memorial.

One regret we had after leaving Williamsport occurred when the pulpit committee traveled early one Sunday morning to hear a candidate for pastor. They had a horrific accident. A drunk driver hit their car head-on and the pulpit committee chairman was killed instantly. Four others were seriously hurt and the church secretary died within a year.

ON TO TEXAS

We loaded a U-Haul with our possessions and with our old Volvo hooked on behind, we headed toward our new destination, excited as young children about to go on vacation.

Tired after four days of travel, but enthusiastic in anticipation of what the Lord had for us, we unloaded the U-Haul and carried our furniture into the house. Our new home was just a block from Madison High School for fifteen-year old Rebecca, and two blocks from ten-year old Joshua's elementary school.

As we were about to unload the last piece of furniture, Evelyn tried to jump from the truck to give me a hand. But her leg caught in a chain and she was thrown to the ground with a broken leg! What a start! Since we did not have a doctor yet, we rushed off to a medical center for her fibula to be set.

Even after her leg was set in a cast, Evelyn made her way to the neighbors to begin our ministry among them. Jose´ and Yolanda, a Hispanic couple who lived across the street, showed friendliness, but Jose´ warned, "Do not to talk about religion because we are Catholic." As our friendship grew, they became less wary of Protestants. Their son, Joseph, became good friends with Joshua. In fact, Jose´ and Yolanda were one of the first couples to attend our neighborhood Bible Study.

All of those who attended were Hispanic. Evelyn also began a Bible Club for the children of the community.

Since we had only about $300 monthly support, we had to find jobs before we had used up all of our savings. For a while, I was a substitute teacher in the high school.

Substitute teachers often provided an opportunity for unruly students to act up. But I had the chance to encourage the youth too. One "class trouble-maker," a slim black boy disrupted one of my classes. Near the end of the period, when the students had completed their work, I gave him permission to tell a joke in class. He did it exceedingly well. After class, I called him aside and spoke of the potential for his life, but told him he had to use it for good instead of wasting his life. I asked him if he had accepted Christ. His answer was "no." I told him, "That is the source of your problem. Think of how the Lord could use your personality for Him, if you become His child." He left, but several minutes later, just before my next class was to begin, he beckoned me out of the classroom and very sincerely thanked me for my advice. When I saw him a week later, he said he had spoken with his Christian grandparents and had accepted Christ. On my way to lunch one day, I saw him listening to tape from his Sunday church service! I wrote, "Even in this supplementary work, the Lord has a use for us."

When I had completed the year, I associated with Century 21 and took four real estate courses. In the six months I worked as realtor, I became the top salesman in our office. Evelyn taught full time in a Christian School and our "tent making" income was a provision of the Lord. By this time, her leg was healed and she had undergone a successful hernia operation. The second year, Evelyn began substitute teaching in different schools all over San Antonio. She used a map to find her way through all the traffic in that busy city.

Pastor Steve Troxel introduced us to several families from Wayside Chapel who were praying about starting a church in the northeast of San Antonio. One couple in particular helped us in any way they could to make us feel at home. Folke Johnson, a member on the District Board, was a happy, gregarious man of Swedish descent and his wife was a sweet, hospitable lady. Another District Board member, retired Chaplain Bob Gower and his wife, Eleanor, also began to be friends.

I felt it was necessary for me to transfer my ordination from the Methodist Church, since I was interested in serving with the Evangelical Free Church of America. When I had put my ordination on hold, I was advised to send in my ordination papers. I wrote to Dr. Montgomery to see if he could help, because the District Superintendent in Texas had questioned the term in the transfer papers, "honorably dismissed." I think the term 'dismissed' concerned him. On September 22, he wrote a letter to Superintendent John Sundstrom, explaining that my letter of transfer, which contained the term "honorably dismissed," was the term used at that time when one discontinued with the Methodist Church. He ended his letter:

> "As long as Mr. Kinzie was affiliated with the Central Pennsylvania Conference, he was a member in good standing, always acquitting himself and his church or

churches commendably. To the best of my knowledge, which admittedly has grown a bit hazy after ten years of retirement, there was never a word of reproach, complaint or criticism concerning Bill's workmanship, personality or conduct. He was respected and admired, as much professionally as socially. Therefore, it is my pleasure to commend William Kinzie to your Board's good graces. Meanwhile, my daughter, The Rev. Joanne Montgomery-Link, pastor of the Epworth Methodist Church, Harrisburg, Pa., and a member of our Conference Board of Ordained Ministry, promises to seek further clarification of the records obtainable."

Following is part, of a letter from Jody:

Dear Bill,

After spending 3 hours today on calling Brian Fetterman, Dick Felty (registrar), Charles Shearer and going over Don Shafer's old journals (the last time you are listed is 1957—then your name drops from sight), I rang the Bishop's secretary and who should answer but the Bishop himself. "Maybe I can help," he suggests, so I presented your case, and he promised to write to your District Superintendent a letter today. Dad sent me a copy of the letter Mother obviously composed. With that epistle, the board probably no longer needs to hear from the Bishop. My mother is someone special!

Jody continued with the encouraging letter and said she was happy to have met our family when we had stopped by

Lycoming College, where she was teaching a special Bible study on Isaiah.

Sometime later, District Superintendent Sundstrom gathered a number of pastors to exam me for the ordination transfer. It all went well, and I was very thankful for the help from the Montgomerys.

About seven men asked me to lead a Bible Study for them in connection with their prayer for a new church. After I taught for several weeks, a school was rented and people were invited to the first service of Northeast Bible Church. Ninety people showed up the first Sunday. I was asked to teach an adult Sunday School class and to preach at times, as the church began to grow.

One man who had initiated the idea of starting a church in the Northeast seemed to be uncomfortable with my presence. I suggested that he and I meet with Pastor Steve Troxel, who had encouraged me to come to San Antonio and to get involved in the forming of a new church. Steve said that he thought this would be a good relationship to include me. I could possibly become their first pastor. This idea did not please the man. I do not know what he was feeling, unless he saw me as an intruder in his project.

I continued to minister there for a short time and helped with their constitution. But then a group from the small town of Boerne, Northwest of San Antonio, asked if I would help them start a church. I began a Bible Study with them, which continued for three months. Rebecca with her friend, Rusty, liked to attend with Evelyn and me. We studied what I called "The Three Pillars of the Church," which every congregation should be built upon. "Faith: teaching the Word of God and looking to the Lord for His leading and control. Hope: looking for and living in the light of His imminent return. Love: experiencing Christ's love as the atmosphere of the fellowship, which surrounds all of the activities of the church. As the people reach out to the lost, love should be the compelling force as they present the Gospel."

On March 28th, the small group and we decided it was time to begin morning services in a rented Christian school. I preached for them for the first four Sundays. The church was growing and they decided to call an interim pastor. Bob and Ann Owens were leaders with Bible Study Fellowship and members of Wayside Chapel. They were fine leaders and Bob had an outgoing personality. Their connection with Wayside would provide encouragement and financial assistance. Later he was called to be the full time pastor. Bob and Ann became good friends and we often fellowshipped over coffee at a local restaurant in San Antonio.

During this time, Evelyn and I helped with summer youth camps for the Evangelical Free Church. I was asked to be a member of the District Board of Education. Rebecca and Joshua helped plan the activities at Twin Oaks Ranch and Rebecca also served as counselor for the children's camp. She and Joshua looked forward each summer to meeting their friends at the Ranch.

Several Roman Catholic ladies and others came each week to Evelyn's Bible study. Her Bible Club was also going well with 18 children present each week. At least 10 made professions of faith.

Besides serving as camp counselor, Rebecca served the Lord by singing duets with Evelyn. As a Child Evangelism missionary, she led several children to the Lord.

Then a church in Pleasanton, a town South of San Antonio, asked me to preach while they were seeking a new pastor. I preached there many Sundays, with Evelyn concluding my message with a Scripture song she composed that fit in with my sermon. The people enjoyed Rebecca and Evelyn singing duets. We were well received. Every time we came to preach, we were invited out to a restaurant and loved the people we fellowshipped with. The leaders asked us to candidate as pastor, but we did not feel led. We replied that we felt God had led us to San Antonio to plant a church.

We had been doing visitation in hopes of planting a church in North Central San Antonio and we were meeting for prayer with Bob and Eleanor Gower and Folke Johnson. We were happy to have such talented people praying with us. I went house to house in the area telling about our interest in starting a church for the community.

At Christmas time, we made a trip to Mexico to visit Doris and Larry and to participate in a Medical Caravan of over two hundred people. There were doctors, anesthesiologists, dentists and support personnel. It took place in a small village in the mountains called Tlauhueteta. To get there, we had to travel over winding mountain roads at the average speed of about 5 miles an hour! At one point, one of the vehicles in the caravan broke down, so we all had to stop. We were in the lead vehicle and had to stop on a curve.

While we waited, Joshua was standing on the edge of a precipice. Then a truck came careening down the mountain and everyone hustled to the opposite side of the road. But Joshua had to stand precariously near the edge of the precipice and the truck miraculously missed knocking him over the edge. We thanked the Lord and knew that He had some future use for Joshua.

At the village, we each had an assignment: Rebecca prepped people for surgery and worked in the recovery room caring for them afterwards, taking and recording their temperature and blood pressure. At one point the doctors tried to save the life of a premature infant, and Rebecca helped hold and comfort the tiny newborn, but he was too small to survive. She also counted out pills and was being taught to give injections. Joshua helped in the kitchen and carried water; Evelyn taught the children on the caravan and I passed out tracts and showed Christian movies in the evening. It was a trip none of us would ever forget. Doris and Larry, who were counted on to find the villages for the caravan ministry, went on medical caravans every summer and every Christmas.

Rebecca was busy in high school. She ran with the cross-country team, was in the choir, wrote for the school newspaper and was in drama. She was voted "Actress of the Year," for her portrayal of "Pipi Long Stocking," the mischievous, red haired girl, in a Swedish children's play.

After graduation, she studied at Word of Life Bible Institute, located at the Ranch where Evelyn had been Bible teacher. She got top grades but did not like the legalism, which was in the extreme. It left her depressed and confused. For her summer assignment, she joined Doris and Larry, her aunt and uncle in Mexico. She served with them on another medical caravan. After coming home, she worked for a while in a little shop and then began studies at the local community college.

There she met Andy Camero, who studied at the Community College. They met regularly before class as friends to discuss items of common interest. I did not approve of him, but they got married, having their wedding in a little church in Barbours, PA, where my mother and dad lived. I performed the ceremony.

1989 Kristian was born, two days after Rebecca's birthday. When Kristian was three years old, Evelyn and I took him to Disney World and then on to Bradenton to meet with the Schirmers. That same year, Andy, who had been unfaithful, sued Rebecca for divorce. After the proceedings, she immediately left for Williamsport, PA and began to study at Lycoming College. While caring for Kristian, she was able to study and graduate in 1995 with a degree in Literature and Poetry. There she met Steve Bastian. He was an artisan, a painter and a craftsman. A poet met an artist! They were married at the beautiful Rose Valley Lake. I performed the ceremony.

In the meantime, Joshua struggled in High School because of dyslexia. His IQ is high and his understanding of the world around him was exceptional. To explain how he felt he used to say, "I'm street smart." When a senior in high school, he was assigned to a work-study program. He was mechanically minded and inventive. He would have had a fine career in a machine shop. Even though I suggested that to his guidance counselor, he was assigned to the Petroleum tower as a waiter. After graduation Joshua wanted to study at Texas A& M, but his dyslexia did not allow him to enter directly. He was to get a foundation at a local community college. Although we paid for his housing, food, tuition and clothes, he felt he had to get a job. This interfered with his studies and when a friend from Mexico, Esther, started corresponding, that was the end of his college career. Esther, who was an accountant, and he were married in Puebla Mexico, where I happily officiated at the wedding. Later they moved to San Antonio.

When the South Central District Superintendent resigned, Bob Gower asked me to candidate for Superintendent. I had never been pastor of an Evangelical Free Church. It seemed unusual that I could be Superintendent with no Free Church background. Reluctantly, I said I would pray about it. Evelyn and I prayed together about what the Lord wanted. I lay awake at night and wrestled with the thought that the Lord had led us to plant a church in San Antonio. The night before the deadline, I called Bob and said, "We came to San Antonio to plant a church, so I must decline." He replied, "As District Superintendent you can plant many churches." That night I had no peace about saying no. Maybe this was why the Lord had led us to Texas. Realizing that there were about six other candidates who had an Evangelical Free Church background, I did not feel that I would be selected anyway, but I wanted to let the Lord make the decision. I called Bob in the morning and allowed him to put my name up.

CHAPTER 22

A NEW CHALLENGE

Another turn in our zig-zag path came when, to my great surprise, I was nominated as the remaining candidate for superintendent. Before the District Conference met, I was asked to preach in many District churches so people could get an idea of who this nominee was. Since the headquarters of the Evangelical Free Church knew nothing of me, Rev. Dean Smith, head of the Church Ministries Department, flew down to San Antonio to meet with me. He wanted to look me over to see if I would be a suitable candidate. Apparently his misgivings were overcome and he gave his approval. Later, whenever the district superintendents met in Minneapolis, he invited me to stay in his home. He was a fine gentleman and a great host.

At the next district conference, I was voted in to be the new district superintendent. I humbly accepted the position. The district covered the whole state of Texas except for the far West part where El Paso is located. In my acceptance speech, I acknowledged that I did not know anything about the job and all I could do was to depend on the Lord who is willing to use weak vessels. As the Apostle Paul said in 2 Corinthians 4:7, "We have this treasure in jars of clay to show that this all—surpassing power is from God and not from us."

My job had three parts: church planting, pastor to pastors, and executive superintendent. I preached in a different church in the district every Sunday and met with the District Board monthly to report on the progress of the district work. I also planned the two biannual district conferences.

The District Highlights was a monthly news bulletin, which we mailed in bulk to all the churches for distribution to the members. Evelyn and I put the bulletin together, printed and assembled several thousand copies and sorted them by zip code for mailing. The purpose of the bulletin was to encourage Free Church people to pray for each other and for the ministry of the District. One feature was to encourage church planting in areas where new churches were needed. It was a great help to small groups praying to start a new church to have others praying for them and even better to have a "mother church" interested in helping with advice and finances. We added to the mailing list the names of other independent churches with the hope that they would join our fellowship of Evangelical Free churches.

Meeting with small groups wanting to start a church, sometimes with no more than three families, was especially exciting. Evelyn often attended and we gave advice and encouragement. When people followed the leading of the Lord and faithfully looked to Him for the increase, new churches sprang up.

Some new starts failed. One, for example, could not agree on the music: some wanted traditional hymns and others wanted contemporary. I tried to help them see that they could use both kinds and that this was no reason not to follow where the Lord had been leading. It was discouraging when they were unwilling to compromise and use both kinds of music. Another failed because some of the group refused to meet in the rented facilities of a Seventh Day Adventist church, as another church plant in San Antonio had done. But the failures were few. From 1980 to our retirement in 1996, 29 new churches were added to the district. That was an increase from 13 in 1980 to 42 in 1994, when we retired.

How we praised the Lord when our ministry among Hispanics began with a small church in Mission, a community along the Mexican border. More Hispanic churches were started along the border, in San Antonio and later in Austin. New flavor was added to our annual and semi-annual district conferences with Hispanics participating. Spanish songs mingled with English echoed through our district camping grounds, Twin Oaks, or through the halls of a host church.

Twice a year we organized the district conferences. Special speakers and musicians added interest to the reports. Sometimes we had various leaders present materials to small interest groups. Reports had to be written about the various ministries to make up the conference minutes. In my report, I tried to show what great things the Lord was accomplishing in our district and to challenge the churches to step out for the Lord.

Our ministry as pastor to the pastors was carried out as I kept in contact with our men by personal visits, arranging meetings of pastors in local areas, and by a monthly letter to each pastor. We held several fun get-togethers in four of the district areas.

Almost every Sunday I preached in one of our district churches. Evelyn used the text of my sermons to write a melody and sang the verses at the end of my message. This was a time for us to get acquainted on a grass-roots level with the people of the district churches. And it provided an opportunity for them to become better acquainted with their sister churches and the district's church planting efforts.

One Sunday as I was preaching, Evelyn's mouth twisted and I looked at her with concern. She waved at me to continue on, but soon fell onto the floor in a seizure. I knelt at her side and prayed, "Oh Lord, please touch this servant of yours whom you love so much and bring her back to me." I did not know what was to come. She was rushed to the hospital and stayed there three days before coming home. I prayed, "Lord, don't let this happen again." But this was the first of four seizures she would experience. At first, the doctors said her seizures were caused by bleeding in a capillary in her brain. Later, they diagnosed the cause as a small calcium deposit in one part of her brain. Her younger sister, Demaris, had had frequent seizures and died of a brain aneurism.

Swimming and fishing on Padre Island, near Corpus Christi was an exciting part of the year for our family. Joshua and Rebecca caught and roasted crabs. We caught a 29 inch Redfish and a huge Grouper, while we waded out into the

Gulf. Joshua and I each had a bag of shrimp hanging at our side and dragging in the water. Later we saw in the newspaper that sharks were swimming around that same area, probably after the same fish we were. Fortunately, they did not want shrimp on that day!

One of the hard parts of my ministry was dealing with internal church problems, when called upon. It was difficult to recommend to a pastor that he resign because he had lost the confidence of his people. Especially heart-rending was the moral failure of several of our pastors. They hurt their families, their churches and ruined their ministry.

Pastors seeking a church sent their resumes to me in hopes that a ministry would open to them. Then when a church was looking for a pastor, I sent them the resumes I had which I felt would fit their situation.

Every year the EFCA district superintendents would meet at Trinity Evangelical Divinity School to interview graduating students for potential ministry in their district. I looked forward to that time of fellowship with these young men who were eager to step out for the Lord. I presented the challenge facing us in Texas, praying that the Lord would lead some of them to us to plant churches. I also spent time at Dallas Seminary to meet and challenge students to serve in Texas. Two Hispanic young men, Alex Mandes and Reuben Martinez expressed an interest in planting Hispanic churches. Reuben successfully planted a church in Edinburg, Texas, an area where he grew up. I counseled Alex to associate with Wayside Chapel in San Antonio where he wanted to plant a church. Wayside acted as a mother church for him. Recently, he has been called to direct the Hispanic ministries for the whole Evangelical Free Church denomination.

After thirty years of marriage, I wrote the following poem:

TO MY BELOVED EVELYN

Thirty years have now passed and gone
 Since I first sent a birthday greeting
To the dearest on earth to me,
 While I longed for our next sweet meeting.
As I said many years ago,
 Life is brighter when I am with you;
God's love seems deeper and aglow;
 Every flower has a deeper hue.
Your walk with God is plain to see
 And your love for others shining through,
Reflects your deep, inner beauty,
 And speaks in all you say and do.
You said, "grow old along with me,"
 As we partners travel side by side,
Adding, "the best is yet to be."
 This you said, my lovely, lovely bride!
The Lord bless you and grant my prayer
 To give you peace, love and joy today.
May you see His hand everywhere,
 As you celebrate this your birthday.

Your loving husband, Bill

When my dad was 90, we received a call that he was very ill and in the hospital. I was unable to come right away because of my work, but Evelyn immediately flew up to help care for him. I spoke to him on the phone while he was in the hospital, but he was soon released. The surgeon had opened him up but closed the incision again because he was too full of cancer to do anything. Evelyn tenderly helped Mother care for him and I took a plane immediately. Unfortunately, he died while I was in flight. At the memorial service, a friend read about how he and Mother moved so many times. He never seemed satisfied until he bought a home and retired in Barbours. She spoke about how everyone who entered the house was invited to a game of Uno.

Evelyn offered to stay with mother for a while. But Ruth and Harvena thought she should live with Ruth, so Mother moved in with her daughter, who lived a half mile away. It was hard for her to leave her home.

Three months later, she became very ill. Doris was in Mexico and did not know that Mother had become so ill so suddenly. Evelyn, Ruth and I were around her bed when she asked for Harvena and Jim, her daughter and son in law. They had traveled to Barbours in their RV and it was parked at the old home. Evelyn offered to drive up to get them. While she was gone, Mother looked up and declared, "Oh, I see the gates opening. And I see Raymond! And I see Harry," her first husband who had been killed in the mines. "I know I shall see Jesus because He promised. Oh! I see Him and He is just as beautiful as I imagined. I just want to kiss His feet." When Evelyn, Harvena and Jim arrived, we all gathered around her bed. She said, "Goodbye Harvena; goodbye Jim; goodbye Ruth; goodbye Bill; goodbye my daughter Evelyn." She and Evelyn had been very close, and it was special that at a time like that she would call Evelyn her daughter. Later that night, Evelyn and I lay beside her bed, listening to her labored breathing. Then it stopped and she was with her Lord.

Mother and Dad had lived Barbours, PA from 1969 until they went to be with the Lord in the Spring of 1992. Doris and I inherited the property and we rented it out for two years. The rent money was divided between Harvena, Ruth, Doris and me. At the end of the two years, when it was time for Evelyn and me to retire, Doris agreed to sell her share. so we could take up residence.

Though it was a fulfilling and often exciting ministry to be involved in what the Lord was doing during those fifteen years in Texas, we had served three four-year terms as superintendent and felt it was time to retire at the age of 65.

Chapter 23

Retirement or Re-tiring

Retirement meant for us: re-tiring; we would put on four new tires and continue serving the Lord. In looking back to our wedding day, Evelyn wrote this free verse poem:

Do you remember the third of September
When we pledged our love to each other?

This gift is far greater than we understand;
It is part of God's planning for man.

That you and I could live our lives on earth at the same time—and together,
How incredible God's plan for his children!

Two are better than one when two become one.
This is God's plan for His children.

Two will not be overcome on this journey we run.
We are stronger and better together.

If I fall down, you lift me up higher.
Sing sweetly, sing softly, sing together.

So we sing together far away and at home;
In hot weather, cold weather too.

If you have cold feet and you cannot sleep,
Just put your cold feet upon mine.

If I have warm feet, I'll put them on thine,
So we'll be much closer together.

The years have gone by; we were young, now we are older.
Turn the pages of life.

Grow older with me; the best is yet to be—
A three-strand cord cannot be broken.

God's Son is the Way, the Truth and the Life.
How incredible God's plan for His children!

After a stirring retirement going-way party by district pastors and leaders, we loaded up a U-Haul, pulled our 1992 Pontiac behind and headed off to our family's homestead in Pennsylvania. Dad and Mother had lived there for almost twenty-three years, and we thought this was a good way to keep the homestead alive. It was wonderful place to retire. It was snuggled in lofty mountains near the beautiful Loyalsock creek in the community of Barbours. By mutual agreement, we had an appraisal made to determine the home's worth. We paid Doris half and began planning how we should remodel this country home.

The homestead needed a lot of work. A bad storm had caused leakage and damage to the house but we got a generous settlement with the insurance company, which gave us a nice sum of money to begin remodeling. Evelyn and I worked hard that first year. Joe, a friend of our son-in law, Steve, did most of the construction work. Steve helped put the new roof on the garage and the breezeway. The metal roof of the house was painted with silver paint. Large double windows were installed in the breezeway to make another room. We had the gravel driveway and garage floor cemented. All the warped paneling was torn down and dry-wall put up. The ceiling in the living room and kitchen had to be replaced. At the same time, we had some wiring done so that all the appliances in the kitchen would have adequate electricity. The entire house was shed of its asbestos siding and replaced with insulation and aluminum siding. All the old windows, upstairs and down, were replaced with double-paned windows.

We redid the back porch, insulated it and put in picture windows to make it into a dining room with a terrific view into the backyard and the dense wood beyond. The upstairs closets were redone with full-length sliding mirrors, making the rooms appear larger. I laid linoleum in the kitchen and in the bathroom. Evelyn and I repainted the walls. A new, forest green carpet, matching the outdoor surroundings, was laid throughout the house. To supplement the outside cellar doors, we cut a new doorway down into the cellar and made stairs so we could enter it from the house. A new furnace and water heater was installed and a 200-amp fuse box replaced the inadequate 100 amps. I rewired the garage to accommodate woodworking machinery. Within the year we had the cesspool dug out and replaced and a new well pump installed. A load of sand was added to filter any ground water that would seep down into the well. These were only some of things we did to redo this house inside and out. It became a lovely country home and a renewed homestead.

Because we wanted to stay active in ministry, we became a member of Interim Pastoral Ministries. We looked forward to helping churches that were in between pastors or were struggling over various issues.

An Evangelical Free Church was just starting in Muncy and we decided to worship there and serve any way we could. Evelyn taught a young people's Sunday School class and I taught an adult class. I preached from time to time and we helped in Vacation Bible schools. Evelyn enjoyed being a part of the skits, and as always, did a superb job. When I was asked by the Methodist pastor in Barbours to fill the pulpit for him, he told me that a district superintendent was Jody Montgomery Link! I asked him to send my greetings at the conference.

For Evelyn's sixty-ninth birthday I wrote the following poem, remembering the time before marriage as we met at Word of Life. The cameo in the poem also called back to 1962, our first conference in Rome, and our first anniversary when I bought her a cameo:

Thirty-six years ago I saw a beautiful cameo!
It was not on a ring
nor on a medallion.
She was walking and talking, so long ago.
What a beautiful thing!
not on a medallion.
Little did I know how beautiful she was,
Inner beauty still veiled,
not as a medallion,
But a living, vibrant soul with a cause,
To see Jesus prevail
not on a medallion.
Her heart's yearning to see men bow at His feet
In humble surrender;
not to a medallion
But to the One who alone can make life complete.

It is difficult to describe my lovely and vivacious wife. As I think of some of the contrasts in her many-sided person, I think of her as:

Tender but tough
Sweet but strict
Free-spirited but disciplined
Beautiful but not proud
Gifted but humble
Stylish but modest

Child-like but mature
Happy but serious
Delightful but dedicated
Dependent but independent

She was the perfect partner for me and it was the grace of the Lord that brought her into my life.

We candidated for Interim Pastor in several churches and the first one we went to was in Jupiter, Florida. Although the congregation was down to about 25 attendees, the buildings were any pastor's dream. The church was located on the main intersection of town with a sanctuary that could seat about 300. An excellent educational building and a large gymnasium completed the picture. Once a week, elderly people from the community were invited to a free dinner and program in the gymnasium. Besides special music, Evelyn and I had the privilege of devotional teaching to the mixed group, a number of whom were Jewish. During the three months we were there, the congregation doubled, a youth group and a men's Bible Study were started. In our usual partnership, Evelyn sang one of her Scripture songs when I finished my sermon. I had the privilege of baptizing three of the new members. Door to door visits brought new attendees into the church. We called it "A church on the move" in pamphlets we printed and on a large banner in the back of the sanctuary. Our plan was to pave the way for the pastor they were looking for. When he came, we sadly moved from our new friends.

The next calling was to a church in Susanville, California. Again the church was dwindling and they had dismissed the pastor. The youth leader was also dismissed because he had had an affair with one of the youth workers. After we were there awhile, one of the elders openly confessed to being hooked on pornography and had to resign that position. We had our work cut out for us. The people of the church were wonderful and cooperative. Evelyn taught Sunday School and again sang her verses after I preached—she sang one of her encouraging verses every chance she got. I preached Sunday mornings and started a Saturday morning Men's Bible Study. We did much visitation and counseling during our stay in Susanville. We attended two Bible studies every week and grew close to the families that met. One of the joys of this kind of ministry was to see the response of the people and the friendships formed. We spent much valuable time with many of the families, visiting in their homes, enjoying dinner and even looking for Indian arrowheads with a family near a lake. We cheered for the football team that one of the high school boys was on and played games with the young people at their meetings. Many of the members joined the community choir singing Handel's Messiah, thrilling our hearts as we prepared for Christmas. The church had provided an apartment for us to live in and we purchased an old car for our use. One of the members bought it back from us when we left.

Before our commitment was up, the newly-called pastor moved to the community and spent our last few weeks with us. He attended my men's Bible class and saw how I conducted it. The day arrived when the days of our ministry were finished and we again, sadly said goodbye to our newly found friends.

Chapter 24

Years in Florida

Evelyn's Parkinson's required her to walk to stay loosened up and maintain her muscle tone. In Barbours, she walked every day to my sister Ruth's home. There they read the Bible, prayed and fellowshipped in the Lord. The round trip gave her a mile and a half of exercise every day. I often walked with her, hand in hand, along the crystal clear Loyalsock creek. Evelyn and I also took long and happy walks together on the wooded mountain trails. We reveled in the beauty of God's creation, the oak trees and towering pines. Birds chirped in the trees and occasionally a deer and her fawn crossed our path. Sometimes we walked up to the Barbours cemetery where Mother and Dad were buried.

I wrote a Mother's Day poem for Evelyn about my love and our walks in the mountains:

"Poems come short of what I want to say.
Words are inadequate my feelings to convey.
'How do I love thee?" does not fully express

The depth of our relationship I want to address.

God's love, so infinite, so eternal, so divine,
Beyond the comprehension of our finite mind
It is beyond man's puny effort to define.
And so is, my Dear, the endless love of mine.

God in His great love gave you to me.
And our life together has been a wonderful key
To joy and fulfillment that He alone could give.
So, let's love and praise Him as long as we live,
And rejoice in the life we share and the love we can give."

Our time in Barbours was happy and fulfilling. However, as the weather got colder, it became increasingly difficult to walk and we decided that we needed to live in a warmer climate.

We approached an Evangelical Free church in Fort Myers, Florida, offering to be Visitation Pastor. We drove down for an interview but decided that the situation was not to our liking. From there, we went on to Bradenton to visit Mr. Schirmer.

Some years before, Mr. and Mrs. Schirmer had retired there. We had visited them several times and liked the beauty of the grounds, the swimming pool and the convenience of the condominiums. Their place faced a beautiful, small lake. The Mall was a stone's throw away, the hospital a five minutes drive and it was only about 20 minutes from the Gulf.

While there, we looked at several places that were for sale. When we saw Apartment 106, Building A, Evelyn said, "This is the place!" We met with the elderly couple that lived there and began negotiations.

Before we put our house in Barbours on the market, Steve and Rebecca showed an interest in buying it. We suggested that Steve get an official appraisal, which he did. We sold it for $10,000 less than the appraisal so that the payments would be no more than the rental house they had in Williamsport. They were happy to have this beautiful setting where both my parents and we had retired.

In August, after we had purchased the condominium, we moved to our new home. Evelyn had hurt her back just before we moved and had to lie across my lap on the seat of our U-Haul truck for the journey.

I had called the local Evangelical Free Church Pastor to see if we could get help unloading our furniture when we arrived in Bradenton. He came with five other men and made short work of unloading the truck. With grateful hearts, we settled in.

For our thirty-ninth anniversary, I wrote the following poem:

"As the sun warms my wind-chilled bones,
Your love for the Lord warms my heart.

As the enchanting refrain of a tender love song
Your singing of the Word thrills my soul.

As the harvest moon reflects the glory of the sun,
Your love for people reflects the glory of the Lord.

To have walked with you through thirty-nine years
Is the next best thing to my walk with the Lord."

I ended with this line: "You have been an inspiration to me and the best help-meet a man could have had. I will praise the Lord eternally for you, my Dear Evelyn."

Evelyn had been putting melodies to Bible verses to memorize them. She produced over fifty Bible songs. As she walked around the 247-unit area, she would stop other walkers and ask if she could sing a verse to them. Many were surprised by this different way of making contact with fellow residents. Her approach was always with a smile and a winsome friendliness and people appreciated her. Her great desire was to reach people with God's Word, and her love for people motivated her. I printed up 8" by 3" cards with her verses and an illustration for her to hand out. She gave out hundreds of cards everywhere she went as she sang the verse. In stores, at doctor's offices and everywhere she could, she gave out cards and sang. One time at the neurologist's office, we had forgotten to take the cards. The receptionist asked, "Where is my card today? I have all the different cards you gave me on our bulletin board here in the office." Later, when Evelyn was gravely ill, Mary Beth, a the Hospice Social worker, was surprised to meet Evelyn. She remarked: "Three years ago, as I was walking on the grounds, I met you. You sang a verse for me and gave me a card. I still have that card in my sun visor and look at it often." Everyone she met was her friend. I think of a poem that she liked: "I want to live in a house by the side of the road and be a friend to man." She dressed impeccably and usually wore a hat. Everything she wore was color coordinated. With her many hats, some called her "the hat lady." Because she served the Lord as she went, some residents called her "the flying nun." We started a Bible study in our home for residents and Evelyn was the greatest recruiter as she met people on her walks!

We loved going to the pool—it provided an opportunity for fellowship with the other residents and I enjoyed the exercise of swimming laps, a total distance of about a fourth mile. Evelyn exercised and enjoyed the jokes and conversation with others. Several times, we went to the Gulf and walked in the sand. She loved looking for shells and weathered glass and then sharing them with others. Sometimes we and a group of our neighbors enjoyed breakfast or lunch overlooking the Gulf. At first, she was able to walk around the units several times, covering up to three miles a day and it was good for her Parkinson's. Several months after we moved in, she had a seizure, the third one in the past six years. The EMS man tied her down to prevent her from moving. This was the wrong thing to do for one who is having a seizure, and as a result of her osteoporosis, her shoulder broke. An X-ray revealed several broken vertebrae and she had surgery called Verteboplasty. When she was under anesthesia, a bone specialist tried to put her shoulder back into place, to no avail. He gave her two alternatives—undergo a severe and painful operation to replace her shoulder or continue with the shoulder out of joint. She chose the latter, even though it meant years of pain. Later she had an operation called Kyroplasty on three more vertebrae. In both operations, cement was put in the broken vertebrae to relieve the pain and to keep her posture erect. After a time of recovery, she was back walking again with a three-wheel walker I had purchased for her. She called it her "MR-2," the name of a sports car she had admired.

I was persuaded to run for Association Board of the condominium and was elected, giving me an ideal opportunity to serve the community. I spearheaded the project to install a geo-thermal heating unit for our pool so people, including Evelyn, could swim even in the winter months. It also led to enormous savings. Rather than heating with expensive gas, the heat source now was extracted from the ground. I also led a committee to rewrite the old Constitution and to bring it up to date. Then I was asked to redo the Rules and Regulations. I was glad to be of service to the Association, but it was difficult with Evelyn's declining health. I hated to leave her and had to have someone stay with her when I attended the meetings. Because of Evelyn's health, I declined to continue after my three-year term.

Evelyn had an artistic bent and beautifully decorated our home. Our large living room was perfect for a Bible Study of up to 20 people. I had stopped going to church because I didn't want to leave Evelyn, so we had our worship service and prayer via TV Sunday mornings, but we both looked forward all week for that Thursday night Bible Study. In a way, that was our church meeting. I led an inductive study and attempted to show how to dig out the real meaning and application of verses. I prepared questions for them to answer and said, "We are all teachers under the Holy Spirit" to encourage them to partake.

I spent many hours on-line learning all I could about Parkinson's disease and ordered many helpful books, which I studied. Sometimes I talked to her doctor about some new medicine or procedure I had learned about. I prepared the best meals she could eat and gave her the vitamins she could swallow or found them in liquid form. For a while we went to Sarasota to a Parkinson's specialist, and later to Tampa to a doctor who had co-authored a book on the disease. We even looked into the possibility of an operation called Electric Brain Stimulation, in which the surgeon places an electrode in the brain. A wire runs down from the incision to a small box on the chest, by which the patient is then able to better control the Parkinson's. But we decided against it because of her seizures. Even to test her to see if she qualified, she would have had to be without her medicine for eighteen hours, which Evelyn said was impossible.

Even though Evelyn's health continued to deteriorate, she took great interest in a large garden plot that was overgrown with cactus-like plants. She wanted to make it look beautiful for our residents since it was in a location where walkers passed by. We dug out the old plants and she designed the bed with many different perennial flowers and plants. I did the digging, fertilizing and watering, but it was her garden! Visiting different nurseries to pick out new plants for her garden made her very happy and she kept adding new plants and trimming back the old ones. Many residents of the complex made remarks about the delightful garden and thanked her, often calling it "Evelyn's Garden."

I often told Evelyn how beautiful she was, but she didn't seem to like to hear it. She was told that she was beautiful all her life, and she seemed tired of the label. One day, I came across a song called "The Rose of Tralee" by William Mulchinoch which in a few words expressed what Evelyn was to me. She liked the part "Truth in her eyes" because it seemed to indicate her love for the Lord. I often sang it to her with a revision because we lived in Manatee County:

> "She was lovely and fair
> as the rose of the summer.
> Yet 'twas not her beauty alone that won me.
> Oh no, 'was the truth in her eyes ever dawning
> That made me love Evelyn, the Rose of Manatee."

I added my poem:

> Roses are gorgeous
> All flowers are too.
> But nothing in creation
> Is as beautiful as you.
> As the song exclaims,
> You are fair as the rose.
> But your inner beauty
> Is the Light that is exposed.
> So Dear, I love you
> For all that you are.
> I'll cherish you forever
> With love nothing can mar."

As Evelyn's strength diminished, I took more and more responsibility for our apartment and daily needs. At one point, as I watched her suffering, I cried out to the Lord: "Why are You not touching her?" Then, I felt that He answered in my heart, "I am, Bill, I am using your hands." The care of Evelyn was my new calling and ministry.

About three years after her first seizure, she had another. A calcium deposit in her brain was said to be the cause. This time she went into a coma, which lasted for three days. Friends who came to visit her thought that she was on her way to Heaven but though I agonized over her condition, I did not feel that way. I was sure she would be with me for a while, in spite of her suffering. I prayed much during that time and visitors often prayed too.

Apparently, she dreamed during that time, because as she lay in a coma, she often giggled. As she was coming out of the coma, she seemed to have hallucinations because, after she awoke, she had some memories of images, and said that she even felt God had been talking to her through her teeth!

After a week in the hospital, we finally returned home, but she soon became ill again and was re-admitted. Heart failure was the diagnosis this time and she was given Plavix, which caused severe bleeding. In the middle bed of a three-bed hospital room, with only a curtain for privacy, she bled and bled into her bowel. Every 15 minutes, she had to get up to get rid of the build up of blood. Thankfully, Rebecca as there to help care for her. There was a shortage of nurses in the hospital, and without her I do not know what we would have done. Rebecca and I feared that she might bleed to death. Only transfusions brought her around after many hours.

A bone sample was taken from her and Myelodysplasia, a pre-cancerous condition of the bone marrow, was thought to be found. Consequently, she had to have frequent blood tests to note the progression. However, after several tests, the doctor said there was now no evidence of the disease. The Lord had answered prayers.

After this ordeal, Evelyn was very weak and the decline of her health accelerated. The County Director of Social Services, provided help with housekeeping. Barbabra, the housekeeper they sent, spent three hours on Thursdays cleaning the house and soon became a friend and Evelyn began counseling her spiritually. In addition to Barbara's help, we were given another aid on Monday, Wednesday and Friday to help Evelyn with her showers. This help was a tremendous benefit, since it relieved me of some of the constant care. It also gave me the opportunity to prepare meals, shop for groceries, do the banking and other duties. After a time of extended negotiation with our insurance company, they provided her with an electric wheelchair to use in the apartment and we thanked the Lord for this blessing. Since she was so weak, she used it regularly. I also purchased a three-wheel scooter for use outside, but she never felt quite safe in it.

One day she visited me in my office, lost her balance and fell breaking her wrist. As usual she was stoic about the pain, even as she declared, "It's broken." After a lengthy stay in the emergency room, she was released. But the break was so severe that they had to put a pin into the wrist. It gave her much pain, adding to her other physical problems.

Making doctor appointments was often a problem. She had frequent appointments with a neurologist, and with an orthopedic surgeon to have the cast on her broken wrist adjusted. She had cataracts removed and later she had to have laser treatments. Frequent trips were made to check her macular degeneration and to get glasses. She often had growths removed at a dermatologist's office. Two teeth were removed for a partial plate to be installed. But a bad case of thrush prevented it from being fitted. Because of her extremely difficult time with constipation, we went for help from several internists. "How can one so faithful be afflicted with so many ailments?" I often wondered. But at the same time, I saw how the Lord used even her suffering to bless others. Her cheerful and God-honoring manner not only blessed those with good health but was an encouragement to many who also suffered. She never complained about these difficult trips and always had a cheery attitude for the nurses and doctors. She loved to sing her verses for them. When she had enough strength, she used her walker. At other times, when she was extra weak, I took her in a wheelchair, though sometimes she was just too week to go and we had to cancel the appointments.

Occasionally, after a visit to the doctor, when she was strong enough, we had the pleasure of eating out, sometimes in the Olive Garden restaurant, sometimes in a seafood restaurant near the Gulf. She loved the change from the kind of food we had at home. It was always a happy occasion when we could spend time together in pleasant surroundings, eating a delicious dinner. We were grateful for these "windows" of strength to get away from the tedious days when she had to stay in bed,

Our grandson, Kristian, always had a warm heart for his Mamoo and Dadoo and we loved him dearly. For the second time since Evelyn's illness, Kristian flew to visit and help us, this time on Spring break. He also wanted us to meet his girlfriend, Tori. Evelyn had told him, "If you come, you must help out and get paid for it." Evelyn had always been good at assigning work. Kristian replied, "That is exactly why we are coming, just to help out, but not to get paid." Our idea was to pay them to cover Kristian's plane ticket, for which Tori had loaned him the money. We didn't like to see him in debt, so we paid them for what they did. Tori was a lovely girl with a winsome personality. She also worked hard, sewing and helping where she could. We were happy to meet her and to know that she had a personal relationship with the Lord.

Vivid in my memory, especially when I hear certain Celtic music, is one sweet occasion. I had read that dancing was helpful for Parkinson's patients and mentioned it to Evelyn. One day, we sat in the living room with some friends listening to a CD of Welsh hymns that Rebecca had sent to us. When the music became lively, Evelyn laboriously got to her feet, and to the delight of all, began dancing a jig! What a heart-warming sight! With the others watching, I ventured to get up and dance along with her. Others joined in. (Now, whenever I hear that Welsh melody, I smile at the memory of Evelyn dancing a jig!)

Since I did not want to leave her alone, I always had to have someone stay with her. We had a lot of help from friends and neighbors. Early in December, toward the end of seven years at the complex, our friend Zoe Bowie, suggested that we approach Hospice. At first, I was reluctant because I thought of Hospice as being present in the last few days of a patient's life.

In spite of my reluctance, I finally decided to call Hospice for an interview. What a joy filled our hearts when she was approved by this wonderful organization. They normally take patients who were expected to live less than six months, but sometimes the patient lives longer. Of course, I felt Evelyn had longer to live than six months. Some of the benefits were: twice a week nurse's visits, the opportunity to call a nurse 24 hours a day in a crisis, and the supply of all of her generic medications. Home visits from the doctor were available when absolutely necessary. Since they also provided help with bathing, they sent an aid three times a week. Later the county helper also came twice a week. Jennifer, an aid who became a very close friend, came from Hospice Monday, Wednesday and Friday. She herself had cancer, but it was in remission, so she was a sympathetic and gentle helper. She put up Evelyn's hair on many of these visits, which meant a lot to Evelyn. In addition, we could call on volunteers for help. The physical therapy she got from Colleen, a talented massage therapist, was beneficial and helped with her rigidness.

Evelyn and the Hospice Chaplain, Cinda, became very close. Singing verses together was her great delight to Evelyn. Cinda also invited a volunteer guitarist, Chuck Cobb to come to sing with them. To Evelyn's great pleasure, the three of them spent two sessions singing her Bible verses. Christmas made it impossible to meet again but after Christmas, Evelyn was no longer strong enough able to sing with them.

Although I took on the responsibility of care for Evelyn because of my love for her and the Lord, it was very taxing. Nights were especially stressful because we had to wake up every two hours to give Evelyn her medication and to help her get up to her bedside toilet. She suffered unbearably from constipation. Day and night, she spent many hours trying to get relief. How my heart went out to her as she struggled. Another terribly bothersome development came with a severe case of thrush. She coughed up phlegm repeatedly for what seemed like hours before she got some relief. It was terribly frustrating to me because I could not help her get relief. William, great protector, is what I wanted to be for her and I gave my life to protect and help her. But I felt helpless at these times. All I could do was to call upon the Lord and try not convey my anxiety to her.

Yet, in all that suffering, Evelyn continued to live up to her name, "Light." She lightened up everyone who entered our door. People came to cheer her up and went away blessed. She tried to make people happy and to encourage them with Scripture when she could sing. On the phone with Kristian, Tucker and Lissette, she taught Bible verses through her songs. When she could no longer sing to visitors, her sweet, smiling countenance was blessing enough. She was the most beautiful woman I had ever seen, but more than that, the love of the

Lord and His Word shone through her eyes and caressed her lips. Truly, the meaning of her name "Light" fit her perfectly.

Every night, I read to Evelyn from the Bible and other devotional books. She enjoyed, too, when for the second time I read through Doris and Larry's book, In the Hollow of His Hand, about their more than forty years as missionaries in Mexico. Usually Evelyn would drop off to sleep while I was reading. Sometimes we would lay snuggled together on our queen-size bed and sing. "It is Well with my Soul" and "He Touched Me" were two of our favorites.

After we came to Florida, Evelyn had written another encouraging and challenging letter to me:

> My Dearest Bill,
>
> God made us one and we never walk alone. We walk with God! I met you on the beach serving God and others. You were walking alone with your head up high, independent and willing to "go with God!" You were on your way by faith to only "God knew where." How exciting—God made us one! In Him we were joined "until death do us part." We have laughed together and cried together. We have worked and played together. We have sung and preached together. Our goal has been to tell the world about our God and Savior (Jesus is His name). We have been together even when we were apart . . . in spirit and truth. For richer or for poorer, in sickness and in health, you have been strong and I have leaned on you, and we could be strong together. "Be strong and very courageous be not afraid, nor dismayed, for the Lord your God is with you." You are the man, the only man

for me—a partner, a friend, a teacher, companion, lover. You have been and are a good father to our children and grandchildren. You have and will teach God's Word to our children, grandchildren and anyone else who would listen. You say, "Are you praising the Lord today?" You love others as yourself. 1 Corinthians 13 tells who you are. You are patient and kind. You are not envious or boastful. You are not proud or rude. You do not keep records of wrongs done to you. You trust, hope and persevere! God's love through you never fails! In our home you have been the best husband, father and friend. You have been a servant of God, an example for all. I'm so glad we can continue to carry on together with God. We can take the opportunities He gives and "make the most of them" is my prayer. We can sing together praising God in Psalms and hymns and spiritual songs—making melody in our hearts to our Lord. We can read and learn and pray together. We can look to Him for His mercy and grace and blessing . . . for sunshine and rain, summer and winter. And during this season of our lives we can emphasize God in our lives. We can stay close to Him and therefore to one another. Think, that God let us live at the same time, become one flesh, work, love and live together for Him, grow old together and see all in this life while we wait to see Him and life hereafter. Then we'll step on shore and call that Heaven. We'll take His hand and continue to go throughout eternity. We'll continue to walk with God!

All my love to the father of my children

Evelyn

The county provided respite for me in the form of four to five hour sessions, Tuesdays and Thursdays, when an aid came to sit with Evelyn. Gwen was a tremendous help to Evelyn and they grew together as close friends. I continued to make meals and saw to it that Evelyn took her medicine every two hours. Gwen would say, "You are not having a respite!" But it did relieve some of the pressure on me so I could tend to other duties. To Evelyn's delight (and mine too) Rebecca, Steve, Kristian and Tucker visited once a year around Christmas time. She loved it too when Joshua and Lissette came annually around the Holidays.

A year or so earlier, I had said to Evelyn, "I wonder how Jane and Jody are doing." To my surprise, she answered, "Why don't you call?" After a little research, helped by Jody, we did call Jane in Tallahassee. I was happy that Evelyn and Jane could meet on the phone. Evelyn enjoyed their conversation and remarked, "I think I could be her friend." When we learned that Jane had bone cancer, I was saddened, knowing what a painful disease that was. My brother-in-law, Clayton Burchill, had suffered long and died of bone cancer. But Jane put a happy face on her experience. She said, "They sent me home to die, but I'm still here! I can even get my walker into the car by myself." Jane offered to send us a photo of herself and her family. We also sent her photos of our family.

Jane noted several parallels in our lives: "You met Evelyn at a Christian camp and I met Joe at the Wesley Foundation. You were married September 1961 and we were married December 1961." She filled us in on what life had brought her and said she was still able to go to church Saturday evenings and Sunday mornings. We told her about our adventures and sent a brochure about the Scandinavian Bible Institute, which we had called a "Miracle in the Making." It was enjoyable to have made that contact again, but I often wondered why I felt such an urge to get in contact after so many years. I hoped that in her illness, contact with an old friend and my sister's book, which I had sent her a copy of, were an encouragement. Later Doris received a sweet letter from Jane saying how much she enjoyed the book. A year later, her husband, Joe Donaldson, called on the phone to say that Jane had died. Jody also wrote, saying, "She was welcomed into Heaven with open arms. She had been very stoic about her illness."

Christmas 2007 was delightful. Evelyn always seemed to respond with added strength when her children visited. Rebecca helped every minute and Steve, Kristian and Tucker pitched in with the work. Joshua and Lissette did too when they came after New Year's Day. They helped so much that I got a little spoiled as they took over some of my duties. From that time on, she gradually got weaker and weaker. At times, she wanted me to call Rebecca and Joshua because she thought she was dying. I felt the weakness was due to "off periods" in her Parkinson's disease. When I called Hospice, they recommended giving her a small dose of morphine or Xanax and to keep the oxygen machine on her. She hated the morphine because it made her even weaker. In retrospect, I believe these weak times were related to her weak heart. Hospice people have said if a person feels that death is coming soon, it usually does. Evelyn no doubt realized that the Lord was calling her home and wanted to be with her children when the time came.

Her birthday came on March 20. I always said, "You bring in the spring." For her birthday I made a card with many different kinds of hats on the cover because of her love for hats. At the bottom of the page, I put a crown representing her reward in Heaven. Inside I wrote my last poem to her:

The years have come; the years have gone
As we have served the Lord.
The wonders of our common bond
Lie hidden in His Word.
You are my Dear, the only one
Who fully warms my heart.
Your love for Him and work you've done
Your life showed from the start.
As we together run this race
We will hold each other's hand
Until we see Him face to face
In the other, awaited land.

One night, five days later, she became extremely weak and her breathing came with a rasping sound. I called Hospice, but because it was night and the only available nurse was 45 minutes away, I said, "I cannot wait and must call 9-1-1." The nurse warned, "If you do, she will not be with Hospice during the time she is in the hospital. Hospice only makes a patient comfortable but does not treat them. You will have to pay the entire bill." "I don't care," I replied, "She must get help."

When we got to the emergency room, the doctor said that she suffered from congestive heart failure. The only reason that she still lived was that the EMS people gave her forced oxygen. He said her oxygen level was only 70%, so low that he did not know if she would make it until morning. She refused to allow them to put a tube down her throat to drain her lungs because she did not want heroic attempts made to save her from going to Heaven. The doctor asked if I wanted her to receive oxygen. "Of course," I replied. So, they forced oxygen into her lungs. The oxygen level stabilized and she was breathing better by morning.

I called Rebecca and Joshua. Rebecca was able to take a flight immediately to be with her. Evelyn spent seven days in the hospital being treated. Though the time in the hospital was very stressful because Evelyn began to experience "Sundowners" and sometimes failed to recognize us, Evelyn, Rebecca and I had a very sweet and fulfilling time together. All three of us snuggled in her bed to eat our meals and talk and Evelyn even talked Rebecca into singing a duet with her for several of the nurses. The sound of their voices carried out into the corridor and soon a small group of listeners had gathered around the bed.

When Evelyn got home, Hospice had a crisis care nurse waiting to care for her. The nurse did not realize the severity of her condition, so she cancelled the crisis care after three days and nights. She thought Evelyn seemed improved enough to not need that 24-hour care.

Now the three of us were alone without a crisis nurse and though we did our best to care for her, her condition began to deteriorate further. Rebecca and I spent many sleepless nights watching over her and trying to help her get comfortable. At one point, she did get a window of strength and wanted to see her garden. I helped her walk out of our condo with the aid of her walker. We reached the garden and Rebecca took a lovely picture of her. Evelyn waved in her typical friendly way and smiled so sweetly. (See the collage.) That was two weeks before she died and it was the last time she visited her beloved garden. Rebecca and Evelyn enjoyed their time together and took many pictures—even some shots with us kissing. They had a lot of fun, posing and laughing for Evelyn's "photo-shoot." We also spent some time planning her memorial service and she supervised the practice of our song, "The Rose of Manatee," which I planned to try to sing in her honor.

Eventually, as Evelyn's health seemed to stabilize a little, Rebecca felt she needed to get back to her family and her job and she flew home, with great trepidation. For the next week, Evelyn struggled along, continuing to use her oxygen but continued getting weaker and weaker. Evelyn's pain was increasing, and when things became especially difficult, I called another nurse, Kate. She said, "We must send her to a Hospice House." The local hospice had no rooms available, so she was taken in an ambulance to a beautiful Hospice House about a half hour away in Palmetto.

Evelyn had repeatedly asked for Tucker, whom she had not seen since Christmas and wanted to speak with him on the phone. She loved Tucker and Kristian and Lissette so much, and wanted them all with her, but she seemed especially concerned about seeing Tucker and he was pining to be with her as well.

When she was extremely weak and could not get up, the aid would say, "We're going dancing. Put your arms around me and hold tight." Then she would "dance" her over to the bedside commode. Happily, the Lord seemed to give Evelyn a few moments of strength, for which I am thankful. One day, I was able to get her into a wheelchair to show her around the beautiful grounds. She enjoyed looking out over a field where horses were playing, and she was fascinated by some strange birds. She even asked me to break off a branch from an interesting plant, presumably to plant in her garden. However, such "windows" were only temporary, and she languished in bed. But, as usual, her spirit was always bright and the staff fell in love with her.

She had longed to see Tucker and to talk with him on the phone. Evelyn loved her grandchildren deeply. She was not only very close to them, she had always been concerned with the spiritual life of Tucker, Kristian and Lissette and taught them many Bible verses set to her melodies.

Realizing the severity of her condition, Rebecca and Tucker flew down while Steve came in their car. Tucker was especially tender as he stood by her bedside. I asked him to go get her some applesauce, which she was able to eat. He was very shy and nervous to go ask something of strangers, but because he wanted to help his Mamoo, he gathered his courage and went. How tenderly he fed her that applesauce.

On the fourth day of her stay at the hospice house she called us all around her bed and asked that we call Joshua and Kristian on their phones. Holding our hands, Evelyn asked each one of us, "May I go home to Heaven? I want to be with my Lord?" One by one, we all said, "Yes." "Then," she said, "I want to spend my last moments in our home in Bradenton."

The Hospice Ambulance took her home, where she lingered for four days. Steve had arrived by car and he picked Joshua up at the Tampa Airport. She was very weak and had to be held upright, but she was able to see her beloved son Joshua one last time, put her arms around him and bless him with her beautiful smile. Not even an hour after he arrived, she slipped into a coma

As she lay in bed, her breathing became increasingly labored, sometimes stopping for a moment, then starting up again. It was a difficult time for all of us. Rebecca slept on the floor beside her bed and sometimes, I crawled into the twin bed beside her, experiencing her labored breathing and wishing I could take some of it on myself. We spoke to her, hoping that she could hear—we had been told that patients in a coma can often hear and understand. Rebecca took over Evelyn's physical care, washing her face, brushing her hair and teeth and giving her Morphine drops when she sounded as if she might be in pain.

On April 19, I spoke with her niece, Roslyn, on the phone—we had been keeping her sisters and brothers appraised of her condition. Roslyn asked me to say goodbye for her and to tell her that she loved her. She said that maybe Evelyn was holding on for me. I know that my dear wife had been concerned about my future after she left me.

I knelt down beside Evelyn's bed and told her, naming them one by one, how her family loved her. When I told her of my love, I also said "Honey, you don't need to hold on for me. Rebecca and Joshua will take good care of me. I will see you in Heaven." Then I left the room. Minutes later, Rebecca came to see her, and she had stopped breathing. She was with her dear Lord!

I crawled into bed beside her until the funeral director came. Rebecca tenderly washed that lovely body and anointed it with Myrrh, Frankincense, Arabian Rose and Sandalwood. It was difficult to see them wrap her in a sheet to wheel her out of the room, but her face was uncovered and she was beautiful! A peace had settled over her.

Months before she died, we had decided to be cremated and to be buried beside my parents, in the beautiful Barbour's Cemetery in Pennsylvania. However, she became concerned as to whether cremation was Biblical. Rebecca spoke to her about it when she was very weak. She replied, "Let's talk about it later." That time never came.

As we discussed the situation, we decided that the modern method of burial was far less Biblical than cremation. The Biblical method was to wrap the deceased in cloth and place the body in a cave. If Evelyn's body were to be buried, it would first have to undergo the distasteful embalming procedure. Then her body would have to be transported to the airport and flown to Harrisburg, Pennsylvania. That was several hours from where the burial would take place. Transportation from the airport would have presented tremendous difficulty. Would we rent a U-Haul to transport the body? Is it legal for us to do so without getting special permission? Would we have to ask the funeral home in Montoursville to drive the hours to Harrisburg and back again? Then, we would have the services of the second funeral director. We would pick out a casket and concrete lining for the gravesite; then watch her precious body put six feet under the ground. To put her body through all this seemed almost like a desecration. We decided that our earlier decision for cremation was the most honorable thing to do. When I die, my cremated remains will be mingled with hers.

We purchased a beautiful wooden box with a mirror inside the lid and a brilliant butterfly on top. This was symbolic of our lovely Evelyn.

Evelyn died on Thursday, and on Saturday we held a Memorial Service for her in the Community Clubhouse. We opened with a song she had requested at our wedding ceremony "Savior like a Shepherd lead us." Rebecca produced a video showing photos from her mother's earlier life until days before she left for Heaven. The video was backed with a song about grace. Then Rebecca gave a wonderful descriptive message about her mother. With Rebecca's help, I sang Evelyn's song," The Rose of Manatee,"—"She was lovely and fair, like the rose of the summer. But 'twas not her beauty alone that won me. Oh no, 'twas the truth in her eyes ever dawning that made me love Evelyn, the Rose of Manatee." Then I had the opportunity to speak of what Evelyn had meant to me during the 48 years I knew her, 47 of which were as husband and wife soul partners. I spoke of the wonderful marriage we had and how much I had learned from her. I tried to describe what a beautiful servant of the Lord she had been, listing all of her qualities. About 100 people packed the auditorium, showing the great affection the residents had for her. She had left a lasting impression on all those she had met and many people took the open-mike to tearfully express their love and admiration for her.

Joshua returned home by air and Steve and Tucker drove home. Rebecca stayed with me for five days to get things in order and to help me pack for my stay with her family in Pennsylvania. I moved in with them, into the same home that Evelyn and I had lived for five years after retirement. Since Kristian was in college, at the University of Arts in Philadelphia, Rebecca and Steve fixed up his room for me. I even had a computer in my room. They had unlimited long distance calling, which was a boon for me since I had so many calls to make. I felt badly to have taken Kristian's room, but Rebecca fixed up a room in the attic for him for when he was home. He loved it and, to my relief, said he would remain there even when I left. "Dadoo, that's your room now, not mine!" Rebecca and Steve went to all lengths to make me feel wanted and at home. Tucker became a pal and their dog Amelie seemed to know I needed some comfort and was always at my side.

We held a second Memorial Service at the Community Baptist Church Saturday afternoon on May 10. Besides the video that Rebecca had prepared, Kristian also showed a slide show of photographs he had taken depicting my care-giving ministry for Evelyn during her lengthy illness. Although it had been almost twenty-eight years since we had been pastor at Memorial Baptist Church, old friends from there came and joined with friends from Community Baptist. During those twenty-eight years, many of our dear friends had preceded Evelyn to Heaven but many others came to honor her.

A month later, Rebecca, Steve, Tucker and I traveled to Georgia to have a memorial service with Evelyn's family. They had tremendous admiration for their loving missionary sister, aunt, great aunt and friend. Her oldest sister, Velma had gone on to be with the Lord shortly after Evelyn died and her brother, Julien had died earlier with complication from Parkinson's disease. Her younger sister, Damaris died years earlier of a seizure. Mildred, Lola and Roslyn, Lola's daughter who was like a sister to Evelyn, were present, as were Evelyn's younger brothers, Earl and Billy. Her niece, Juanita and her husband Kent, opened their large home and about a hundred people marveled at the life of commitment and love for the Lord that Evelyn represented to them. The memorial service and the testimonies of her loved ones were a stirring celebration of a life well spent.

In July, we held a memorial service in San Antonio, TX, where Joshua, Esther, Lissette and Doris and Larry lived. The families—children, grand children and great grand children—reminisced with love about what Evelyn meant to them. Some related how she had sung Bible verses to them, had them learn the Bible verses and, when successful, reach down into the "grab bag" for a prize.

Joshua wanted me to go with his family for five days to Cancun for a rest and relaxing time. We had a great time together, sightseeing, fishing and eating amazing meals! I stayed for a month with his family and with Doris and Larry before returning to Pennsylvania.

Rebecca, Steve, Tucker and Kristian showed me such love that I was tempted to make Barbours my home residence.

However, after eight months, I had to go back to Florida to see how returning to our condo, with all it's memories, would be. When I arrived, it was like coming home. This had been our home for nine years and vivid memories of the time I spent with my beloved "Rose of Manatee" compelled me to stay. I would be able to travel from Florida to visit in Pennsylvania and Texas. Interim Pastor Ministries could still be an option for me to continue in ministry. The Lord gave Evelyn and me a wonderful life that we would never change for any other life. Both of us gave up our secular dreams of popularity, fame and fortune to answer God's call. Evelyn would no doubt have become a famous actress had she not received the Lord and used her gifts to serve Him. With Ceramic Engineering becoming so vital an occupation, I would have probably fulfilled my selfish dream of wealth and maybe even renown. Neither of us would have traded those dreams for the life the Lord gave us.

He promised us in Proverbs 3:5,6: "Trust in the Lord with all your heart, and lean not to your own understanding. In all your ways acknowledge Him and He will direct your path." KJV. The last part of a poem we wrote for a Christmas card is:

> To Heaven from Earth,
> We're on our way there.
> Though we have no worth,
> His great grace we share.
> In Heaven we'll sing

And give Him our praise—
Forever our King,
The Ancient of Days!

Evelyn and I had followed the zig-zag path led of the Lord before we met. Then, together, we followed the Lord's path for forty-eight glorious and fulfilling years. I would not change any of it if I could.

Evelyn has reached the Summit. I long to be there too. In the meantime, this is my prayer:

"Here I stand, Lord,
Waiting to hear Your voice
Here I stand, Lord,
I have no other choice.
You alone, Lord,
Can answer my heart's prayer.
You alone, Lord,
Can lead me anywhere.
Here's my hand, Lord.
I reach it out to You.
Here's my heart, Lord.
Please search it through and through.
Cleanse and fill me,
With Your Spirit Divine.
Direct my steps, Lord,
And make me wholly Thine.

Swedish Bible Institute Director Takes Pastorate

REV. WILLIAM R. KINZIE

Pastor at Memorial Baptist Church; Evelyn at the Hospital; at my parent's home; the Johansons; Evelyn with her choir; Evelyn's Bible study group; My Mother and Dad.

First church plant that we helped; presenting an ordination certificate to George Billingslea; start of Hispanic church; a pastors' meeting; "Love you, Mamma!"; Joshua; "Slim"; Rebecca as Pippi.

Our remodeled home in Pennsylvania; Evelyn's garden; a girl I can carry; a great sense of humor; on our walks: baptisms at Jupiter, Florida; Susanville, California fellowship; new pastor

Joshua & Esther's wedding; Joshua & Esther; Mary Ellen, Evelyn, Bill, Ruth, Jim and Doris at Joshua's wedding; Steve & Rebecca; Rebecca, Steve, Bill and Kristain at Steve and Rebecca's wedding.

Evelyn and Kristian; Lissette and Bill; swimming with Mary Ellen Mahoney; Among the flowers; Lissette, Tucker, Rebecca Evelyn and Joshua; Birthday with Tucker and Kristian; "I love you Mama;"Tucker, Steve, Kristian, Rebecca; sweet conversation; Good friend Jane.

Singing "Once Upon a Dream"; last kisses; looking toward heaven; fish dinner on the Gulf with friends; last goodbye; a year before Evelyn's last birthday; The Rose of Manatee.

APPENDIX

We climbed the height by the zig-zag path
And wondered why—until
We understood it was made zig-zag
To break the force of the hill.
A road straight up would prove too steep
For the traveler's feet to tread;
The thought was kind in its wise design
Of a zig-zag path instead.
It is often so in our daily life;
We fail to understand
That the twisting way our feet must tread
By love alone was planned.
Then murmur not at the winding way.
It is the Father's will
To lead us home by the zig-zag path
To break the force of the hill.

Anonymous

This is the verse Evelyn most liked to sing. It was used to encourage hundreds of people:

> "Do not let your hands hang limp.
> The Lord your God is with you.
> He is mighty to save.
> He will take great delight in you.
> He will comfort you with His love.
> He will rejoice over you with singing.
> Do not let your hands hang limp."
> Zephaniah 3:16,17; NIV

Since writing these memoirs, I have moved in January of 2011, to San Antonio, where I am enjoying fellowship with Doris, Larry, and their extended family and occasionally, have the pleasure of seeing Joshua, Lissette and Esther.

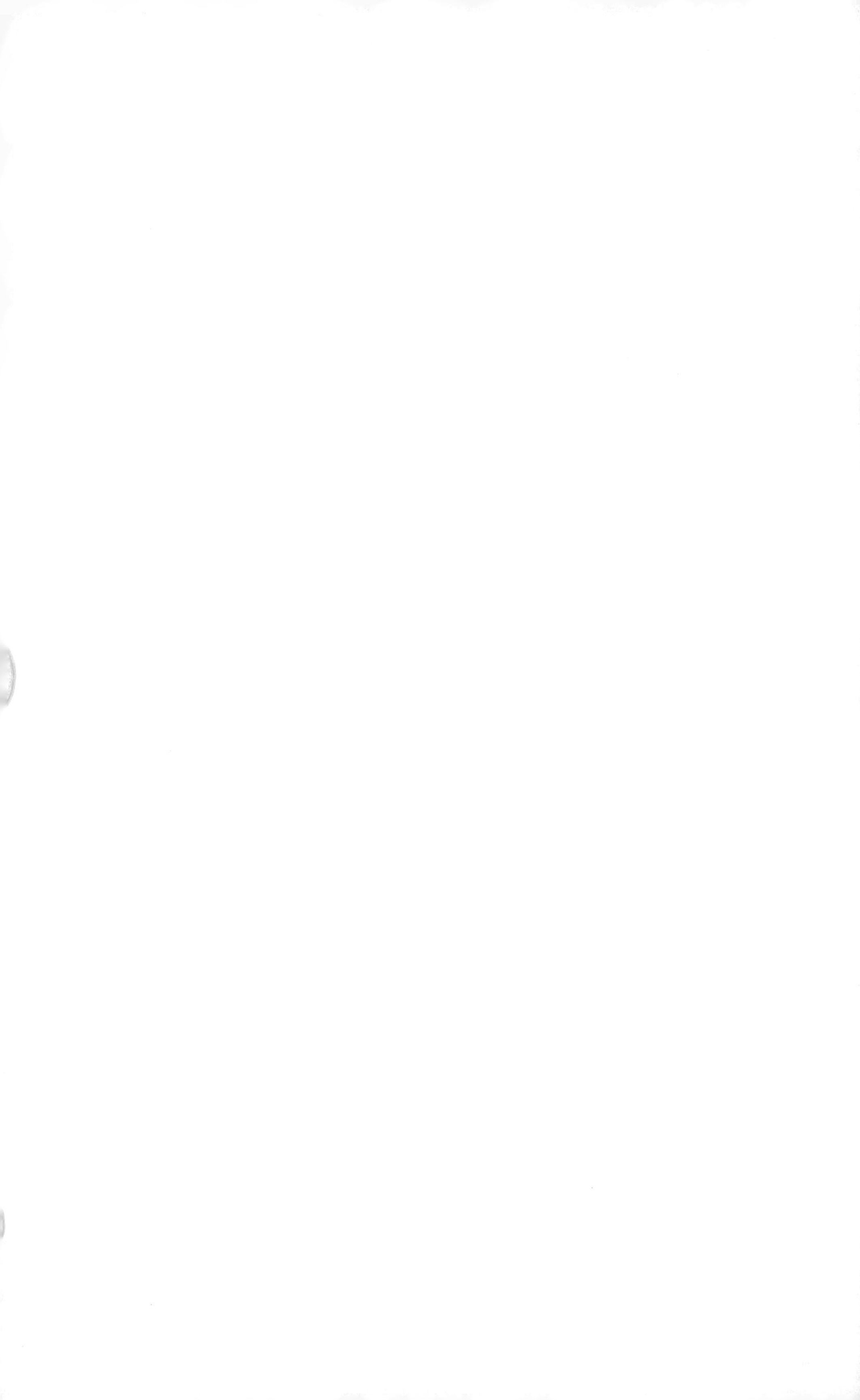